Who Am I?

AvanchaK is a serialpreneur, marketing & strategy expert, and an avid reader. He has been associated with some of the top-notch organizations and has proven himself consistent in enhancing their content by improvising their engagement strategies.

His knack for picking and understanding the latest technologies and trend combined with his fluid reading ability makes him an undebated individual for details and ideas to implement open source technology. His articles are always packed with data and real-life examples. When he is not on the computer, he loves traveling and spending time with his family.

Reset Rethink Reposition

This may be one of the most common problems that a marketer could like face many times in their line of work or not face at all but has been one of the biggest debacles which have claimed one of many marketers careers, it is the very loss of consumer/customer interest in your main product line or services. Most of the time marketers are either late to realize this or they are just not ready to accept this fact. The customer decides on many occasions and due to many not so relevant reasons that one of the main cash cows or best product/service line is not something he/she would not want to indulge into.

This book will deep down on what steps to take to understand when one such situation arises, how you could measure your efforts and the red flags to look out for to avoid this debacle with how to counter this situation or put the life back in your dying product or service line. The mantra that this book intends to propagate is to '**Reset Rethink and Reposition**'. This is quite simple if you intend to think about it but this book is going to deep down on some of the legendary Marketers who were faced by this dire circumstance and who emerged victorious over this situation using the mantra this book intends to propagate.

This book is dedicated to all the marketers or all those who want to get into marketing. This book is also dedicated to all those wonderful people who helped me understand the most important lesson in my life which was that life never stops giving us puzzles but we just need to Reset, Rethink and reposition our thoughts to solve the problem that life has for us. A special token of thanks also goes to Vikram Parekh sir who during my early MBA years ensured that all those who study at ITM would get the privilege of studying with some of the best case studies and whose repeated efforts to help us understand the topic has helped us all get in better positions in our careers & life.

There was once a great king who gave his dynasty a very sane advice, he told them that if faced by the raging sea and you feel that you are losing then just turn around and go with the flow. In life too, if you feel that if life is starting to win while you keep losing then just turn around and go with the flow. This helps to build back some of the confidence and also lose some of the self-doubt and self-criticism. To win in life sometimes all you need to do is reset your position or thought, rethink or clear some of your thoughts/aims and lastly but not the least important step is to reposition yourself with new vigor & thought to win once more.

This book will cover with the below flow in mind:

1. Who AM I? & why you should read this book? – Covered earlier

2. Introduction – Covered earlier

3. The Mantra – Will deep down almost immediately with some easy tips and examples

4. How to find whether to use a mantra or not – Will introduce to some of the tools and markers

5. The analytics – Will introduce to you some of the basic red flags to look out for

6. Some Practical Examples

7. Parle G – How Parle-G fought the thought of price change & emerged as a distinctive brand.

8. Godrej – How repositioning their brand brought forth a new product

9. Tata Ace – How their values & research with a dire need to surpass customer expectations brought a new product line

10. How to implement the mantra

11. What to measure to see if the mantra is working or not

12. Some strategies that brands could employ with this mantra

13. Book Reviews.

Godrej a study of how to not re-invent the wheel but understand your customer requirement and re-purpose your earlier offering to do better.

At the present time in excess of 20,000 multinationals are working in rising economies. As per the Economist, Western multinationals hope to discover 70% of their future development there—40% of it in China and India alone. Be that as it may, if the open door is tremendous, so are the deterrents to seizing it. On its 2010 Ease of Doing Business Index, the World Bank positioned China 89th, Brazil 129th, and India 133rd out of 183 nations. Outlining the bank's decisions, the Economist wrote, "The just way that organizations can thrive in these business sectors is to cut expenses persistently and acknowledge overall revenues near zero."

Indeed, the difficulties are huge. In any case, we couldn't differ more with that assessment. We have seen the chances without bounds on a road corner in Bangalore, in a little city in focal India, in a town in Kenya—and they don't expect organizations to swear off benefits. At first glance, nothing could be more common: a clothing, a reduced ice chest, a cash exchange benefit. In any case, take a gander at the organizations behind these contributions and you will discover the wildernesses of the plan of action development. These novel endeavors uncover an approach to enable organizations to escape stale interest at home, make new and productive income streams, and find the upper hand.

That may sound excessively idealistic, given the trouble Western organizations have had entering developing markets to date. In any case, we accept they've battled not on the grounds that they can't make practical contributions but rather in light of the fact that they get their plans of action off-base. Numerous multinationals essentially import their local models into developing markets. They may tinker at the edges, bringing down costs—maybe by offering littler sizes or by utilizing lower-cost work, materials, or different assets. In some cases, they even outline and fabricate their items locally and enlist nearby nation chiefs. Yet, their major benefit equations and working models stay unaltered, dispatching these organizations to offer generally in the most astounding wage levels, which in most developing markets aren't sufficiently huge to create adequate returns.

What's frequently absent from even the savviest of these endeavors is a precise procedure for reconceiving the plan of action. For over 10 years, through research and our work in both develop and developing markets, we have been building up our plan of action advancement and usage process (see "Reinventing Your Business Model," HBR December 2008, and "Beating the Odds

When You Launch a New Venture," HBR May 2010). At its most fundamental level, the procedure comprises of three steps: Identify an imperative neglected job a target client needs to be done; blueprint a model that can achieve that activity gainfully at a cost the client will pay; and carefully implement and develop the model by testing basic suspicions and changing as you learn.

Begin in the Middle

Built up organizations entering developing markets should take a page from the technique of new businesses, for which all business sectors are new: Instead of searching for extra outlets for existing contributions, they ought to distinguish neglected necessities—"the occupations to be done" in our phrasing—that can be satisfied at a benefit. Developing markets abound with such occupations. Indeed, even the fundamental needs of their extensive populaces may not yet have been met. Truth be told, the test lies less in discovering employments than in settling on the ones most suitable for your organization to handle.

Developing markets abound with "occupations to be finished." Even the essential needs of their huge populaces may, in any case, be neglected.

Numerous organizations have just been baited by the guarantee of benefits from offering low-final results and administrations in high volume to the simple poor in developing markets. What's more, top of the line items and administrations are broadly accessible in these business sectors for the specific rare sorts of people who can bear the cost of them: You can purchase a Mercedes or a clothes washer, or remain at a decent inn, anyplace on the planet. Our experience proposes an unquestionably encouraging spot to start: between these two boundaries, in the huge center market. Buyers, there are characterized less by a specific pay band as by a typical condition: Their necessities are being met ineffectively by existing low-end arrangements since they can't bear the cost of even the least expensive of the top of the line choices. Organizations that devise new plans of action and contributions to more readily address those shoppers' issues moderately will find huge open doors for development.

Take, for instance, the Indian purchaser durables organization Godrej and Boyce. Established in 1897 to offer locks, Godrej is today a differentiated maker of everything from safes to hair color to coolers and clothes washers. In workshops we directed with entering administrators in the machines division, coolers developed as a high-potential territory: Because of the cost both to purchase and to work them, conventional blower driven iceboxes had infiltrated just 18% of the market.

The primary thing these supervisors needed to know, normally enough, was "Could Godrej give a less expensive, stripped-down variant of our higher-end fridge?" We requesting that they consider rather the key needs of those with poor or no refrigeration. Did they know what those purchasers extremely needed? In a word, no. A little group was doled out to direct nitty gritty perceptions, open-finished meetings, and video ethnography to enlighten the activity to be improved the situation that undiscovered market.

The semiurban and rustic individuals the group watched normally earned 5,000 to 8,000 rupees (about $125 to $200) multi-month, lived in single-room homes with four or five relatives, and changed living arrangements as often as possible. Unfit to bear the cost of traditional fridges in their own homes, they were managing with the public, normally used ones.

The common refrigerators weren't addressing these individuals' needs exceptionally well, yet not for the reasons one may anticipate. The eyewitnesses found that they perpetually contained just a couple of things. Their clients tended to shop every day and purchase little amounts of vegetables and drain. Power was untrustworthy, putting even the little sustenance they wanted to safeguard in danger. Likewise, in spite of the fact that they needed to cool their drinking water, making ice wasn't work for which these individuals would "employ" a cooler.

The group presumed that what this gathering expected to do was to extend one dinner into two by safeguarding scraps and to keep drinks cooler than room temperature—a vocation notably unique in relation to the one higher-end fridges do, which is to keep a vast supply of perishables available, chilly or solidified. Plainly, there was no motivation to spend multi month's compensation on a regular cooler and pay soak power costs to complete the less difficult activity. What's more, similarly as obviously, the arrangement was certifiably not a less expensive customary ice chest. Here was a chance to make an on a very basic level new item for the underserved center market.

It's simpler to contact individuals who are now burning through cash to complete employment.

Focusing on this market has two incredible focal points. In the first place, it's less demanding to overhaul the answer for a vocation people are as of now endeavoring to do than to make adequate client request where none yet exists—as would-be sellers of filtered water and other apparently fundamental contributions have found sadly. Second, it's simpler to contact individuals who are as of now burning through cash to complete their occupations. That is basically what Ratan Tata did with the $2,500 Nano. He didn't ask, "How might I get individuals who've never purchased any type of transportation to purchase an auto?" He asked, "How might I create a superior option for individuals who contract engine bikes to transport their families?" The objective is to divert existing interest by offering an unmistakable way from an unsuitable answer for a superior one.

Offer Unique Benefits for Less

To divert request, your client incentive (CVP) must take care of an issue all the more adequately, basically, accessible, or moderately than the options. In creating markets, we have discovered, the segments of a CVP that issue most are reasonableness and access. How about we take a gander at each thusly.

Moderateness.

Western organizations realize that they have to think of lower-cost contributions in developing markets, yet they time and again confine themselves to giving less to less. In 2001, for example, a 300 ml container of Coke cost 10 rupees—multi day's wages, by and large, and an extravagance the organization assessed just 4% of the populace could bear. To come to the next 96%, it presented a 200 ml container and cut the cost down the middle, shaving edges to make Coke more aggressive with basic options, for example, lemonade and tea.

We would say, however, an unquestionably vigorous way to deal with making a reasonable developing business sector offering is to exchange off costly highlights and capacities that individuals don't a requirement for more affordable ones they do require. To get that privilege requires an unmistakable comprehension of the setting in which the offering will be sold—which calls for advance hands-on work, ideally of a community instead of a just observational kind. This is a great item advancement guidance in any market. Truth be told, it applies to indigenous players working near and dear, as Godrej, and in addition to Western organizations going up against the new.

Godrej's group planned and assembled a model cooling unit starting from the earliest stage and tried it in the field with customers. At that point, in February 2008, in excess of 600 ladies in Osmanabad, a city in India's Marathwada locale, assembled to take part in a cocreation occasion. Working with the first models and a few others that had tailed, they teamed up with Godrej on each part of the item's plan. They helped plan the inside courses of action, made recommendations for the top, and gave experiences on shading (at the end settling on treat red).

The outcome was the ChotuKool ("minimal cool"), the best opening unit that, at 1.5 x 2 feet and with a limit of 43 liters, has enough space for the couple of things clients need to keep crisp for multi-day or two. With just 20 (as opposed to the

Parle Products a Discovery of how to use the mantra correctly:

In 2009, Parle Products Pvt. Limited (Parle), a leading Indian biscuit manufacturer, had the distinction of producing the largest selling glucose biscuit brand by volume in the world, the Parle-G. Parle-G biscuits sold for approximately US$1 per kilogram and as very few processed and ready-to-eat foods were available at this price point, Parle-G was strongly associated with offering value for money (VFM). A looming problem in this brand category for Parle was that the input prices of two major raw materials for the Parle-G biscuits (which together accounted for 55 percent of their input costs) had risen enough in the past 18 months to decrease margins from 15 percent to less than 10 percent. Pressure to restore margins led Parle to consider a price increase yet a previous attempt had caused a dramatic reduction in sales. Parle subsequently addressed rising input costs by reducing the weight of the package, franchising production, reducing supply chain costs and reducing packaging costs. Parle could not ignore the deeply entrenched perception of VFM when devising both short- and long-term marketing plans to retain Parle-G's success in the marketplace. These plans needed to address segmentation, positioning and changing Indian demographics when considering a potential price increase for Parle-G biscuits.

In December 2009, Pravin Kulkarni, general administrator, Parle Products Pvt. Ltd. (Parle), a main Indian scone producer, confronted a troublesome choice including the potential cost increment of the organization's leader glucose roll mark, Parle-G. The information costs of two noteworthy crude materials, sugar and wheat flour, which involved 55 for every penny of assembling costs, had ascended amid the previous year and a half. Thus, the edges of Parle-G had diminished from 15 for each penny of income to under 10 for each penny. The strain to restore edges to 15 for every penny drove Kulkarni to consider raising the cost of Parle-G rolls. Since Parle-G's presentation in 1939, the roll mark had been emphatically connected with offering an incentive for money1 (VFM), a commercial center recognition that had stayed resolute for over 60 years. Truth be told, the VFM recognition was related with Parle-G bread rolls as well as had come to characterize the whole glucose scone class. Parle-G was sold to purchasers in 46 stock keeping units (SKUs) at 12 value focuses (see Exhibit 1). The normal cost of Parle-G was around US$1 per kilogram. For instance, a parcel of 15 bread rolls weighing 82.5 grams (g) sold at a greatest retail cost (MRP) of INR4.00 (US$0.08).2

Worldwide, not very many handled and prepared to-eat nourishment things were accessible for US$1.00 per kilogram. Indeed, even the makers of new glucose roll items were compelled to tow this value line to be insignificantly focused in the item classification. Parle had the refinement of having kept up the US$1.00 per kilogram value point for Parle-G since 1990.3 truth be told, VFM was the shopper recognition that had driven Parle-G to end up the biggest offering roll mark by volume on the planet in 2002,4 as approved by an investigation by worldwide statistical surveying firm A C Nielsen. That best positioning had since been held by the brand.

In January 2004, in its first endeavor in 13 years to counterbalance increasing costs, Parle had climbed the cost of its 100-g bundle of 16 bread rolls, from INR4.00 to INR 4.50. The 100-g parcel was Parle's top-rated SKU, adding to 50 for each penny of brand incomes consistently. The thought was to try things out with the main SKU before expanding the costs of different SKUs. The organization needed to move back the expansion rapidly, be that as it may, in light of the fact that offers of the 100-g bundle dropped by more than 40 for each penny inside a half year. The negative customer response was unconstrained and across the nation, driving Parle to reestablish the past estimating of its

Parle-G rolls. After four years, the administration took healing measures to bargain by and by with increasing expenses. This time, Parle concentrated particularly on diminishing the weight, or grammage, of the 100-g bundle. This decrease was done in stages — first, from 100 g to 92.5 g in January 2008, at that point to 88 g in May 2008 and to 82.5 g in January 2009. The number of bread rolls was additionally diminished from 16 to 15. Shoppers saw these progressions; in any case, as long as the organization did not tinker with the value, purchasers appeared to oblige the grammage decrease. Said Kulkarni: Biscuit is a consistent utilization thing in the general nourishment crate which includes 49 for each penny of the financial plan of an Indian family. There is a general propensity among buyers wherever to search for deals while looking for nourishment classes. That clarifies the value versatility of interest in India for bread rolls by and large. Value versatility is especially pervasive in the glucose class of rolls. It wins among all classes of both urban and provincial customers. Not at all like the "liberal" assortment of bread rolls devoured just once in a while, the "useful" assortment of glucose scones is a staple eating regimen among Indian urban purchasers. A few classes of urban customers utilize it as a supplement amid both breakfast and lunchtime. Some utilization it as an every day wellspring of nourishment and calories. For all classes of rustic customers, glucose bread rolls are a noteworthy wellspring of vitality and sustenance. Indian customers wouldn't fret the costs of premium rolls going up. Yet, with glucose class, they are valued delicate. That is the reason I need to continue with caution.5 notwithstanding diminishing the grammage crosswise over SKUs, the organization had attempted cost-control measures to protect edges. For instance, Parle had conveyed fabricating focuses nearer to the wholesalers by diversifying creation in order to lessen dispersion costs. The organization had likewise solidified purchasing and went into forwarding contracts with sellers of crude materials to diminish store network costs. Moreover, the wax-covered paper had been supplanted by bi-pivotally arranged polypropylene (BOPP) paper to lessen bundling costs. The organization could go just so far by utilizing such measures. A cost climb appeared to be a need to reestablish edge levels, especially in light of the fact that the organization had increased its own assembling limit by 10 for each penny on a speculation of INR500 million out of 2008.6 A climb in cost could expand the edge of Parle-G by 50 for every penny and to maybe reestablish it to the prior level of 15 for every penny. However, in the event that the experience of 2004 was any sign, customers would be amazingly touchy to a value climb. Kulkarni was gotten in a predicament.

INDIAN BISCUIT INDUSTRY India was the third biggest maker of bread rolls on the planet, after the United States and China. Despite the fact that 15 for every penny of Indian scone creation was traded, local interest for rolls energized industry development. Roll producing was isolated into two areas — sorted out and disorderly. The previous comprised of 60 for each penny of the national market. The sloppy segment, containing mother and-pop foundations and taking into account the markets of the rustic inside, did not have simple access to bank credit, innovation, and data frameworks. This part was added to a great extent outside the national factual information pool. Development in the Indian scone industry was to a great extent natural in light of the constrained degree for the union in the sorted out division. Low-evaluated assortments governed in the provincial markets where players in the disorderly division had set up passage hindrances for marked scones. In examination with most marked partners, a few times each day, rivals in the country advertise gave neighborhood stores crisply prepared bread rolls that conveyed the smell of novelty, in a whole, and without powder shape. These country contenders and neighborhood retailers had grown long-standing connections that marked players couldn't without much of a stretch change. In the composed part, the five principle classifications of scones were glucose, Marie, sweet, cream and drain. Glucose was a high-volume, low-edge bread classification that spoke to 42 for every penny of the scone advertise and was joined by solid shopper desires for low value focuses. Sweet, cream and drain were "liberal" classes that conveyed premium costs. Marie was an in the middle of class, utilized generally at break time. Parle-G was a piece of the glucose class. The development procedure of all roll majors was to anchor the relocation from the section level glucose class to the liberal classifications. The last was accessible at value focuses starting at INR5. The sorted out part created 1.7 million tons of bread rolls per annum, esteemed at INR110 billion out of 2008. The part was developing at a normal yearly rate of 15 for every cent.7 The rate of development of individual classifications differed. Low-estimated classifications customarily developed at a higher rate than premium classes. Generally, notwithstanding, the top-notch classifications, which truly had developed in the scope of 8 to 10 for every penny every year, we're not just making up for lost time to the rate of development of the low-evaluated classifications, however, were moving into a range simply over the 20 for each penny extend. This upward development was predictable with some positive factors in the Indian economy. An investigation by McKinsey Global Institute, discharged in May 2007, demonstrated that the salary levels of family units in India were ascending, just like the utilization levels of numerous merchandise and administration classes.

Concentrating on nine noteworthy utilization classifications (counting sustenance items) and 30 subcategories, the examination reasoned that the level of spending on optional things would develop drastically, though the spending on essential necessities would develop more slowly.8 The investigation grouped Indian customers into five classifications based on singular yearly wages: globals (those winning above INR1 million for each annum, nearing normal universal measures), strivers (those acquiring somewhere in the range of INR500,000 and INR1 million for every annum), searchers (those procuring somewhere in the range of INR200,000 and INR500,000 per annum), aspirers (those gaining somewhere in the range of INR90,000 and INR200,000

per annum) and denied (those acquiring under INR90,000 per annum). The searchers and the aspirers together framed the working class and were the foundation of utilization for an assortment of items and administrations in India. The investigation demonstrated that the number of buyers in the denied classification would decrease, while the total wage levels of the Indian white collar class would increment, together prompting a four-overlay climb in total utilization (see Exhibit 2). Organization BACKGROUND In 1929, Parle had begun its tasks as a maker of confections in rural

Mumbai in western India. After 10 years, it enhanced into making bread rolls. The organization conveyed cutting edge apparatus that gave programmed printing and bundling, and its bread preparing broiler was the biggest in Asia. Parle had 10 fabricating destinations of its own, notwithstanding 60 contract producing offices, situated crosswise over India. As far as administrative center, the bread showcase was making strides at Parle, to some extent since it was a bigger market than confectionery.9 The organization had 40 for every penny offer of the aggregate scone advertise in India and 15 for each penny offer of the aggregate confectionary advertise in India. A considerable lot of Parle's items were seen as offering great incentive for cash and were advertise pioneers in their separate classifications. Parle recorded a compound yearly development rate of 15 for every penny.

Tata's Lead the way with the mantra:

The Tata Ace

Over the most recent 40 years, we made the ability to assemble 400,000 vehicles for each year. In the following five years, we plan to twofold that. We trust we are at a remarkable time in our organization's history. Keeping in mind the end goal to produce the development we imagine, we should think inventively and create extraordinary items like the Ace.

— Ravi Kant, Managing Director, Tata Motors

The Tata Ace was a little four-wheeled business vehicle propelled by Tata Motors in May 2005 at a cost of 225,000 rupees (Rs.) ($5,000)1with a payload limit of 0.75 tons2(seeExhibit 1for a photo of the Ace). The Ace cost half not as much as some other four-wheeled business vehicle in India and was fundamentally less expensive than pickup trucks with comparable payload limits found in global markets. Not at all like other business vehicles, the Ace, with its smaller size and shorter turning span, could move through India's thin urban avenues and cost-adequately transport little loads to towns and towns in provincial regions. Before the dispatch of the Ace, the little load transport portion was served by three-wheeled vehicles known as auto rickshaws (seeExhibit 2for a photo of a run of the mill business auto rickshaw). Be that as it may, three wheelers were loud, dangerous, and moderate and could topple while conveying large payloads.

By offering a specialty vehicle that met the one of a kind needs of the Indian transportation part at a cost equivalent with that of a three-wheeler, the Ace made a completely new item class (likened to Chrysler's acquaintance of the minivan with the U.S. showcase in 1983) and was a moment hit with people in general. The early focus of 30,000 vehicles was sold in under a year, in spite of the item's being accessible in just roughly 25% of the nation. In October 2005, energized by this achievement, the companyannouncedthatitwoulddoubleannualproductionto60,000units.InJanuary2006,these won BBC Top Gear's yearly "Best Commercial Vehicle Design" award.

Kant was satisfied with the achievement of the Ace, however, he likewise realized that the Tata Motors Board of Directors might want to know his gets ready for expanding on the Ace's prosperity going ahead. With short of what multi-week until the point that the following executive gathering, he pondered what he should recommend.

Review of the Indian Commercial-Vehicle Sector

In 2005, the Indian business vehicle division included three-and four-wheeled vehicles. (Bikes, mopeds, and bikes) and additionally, traveler autos and sport utility vehicles (SUVs) were likewise sometimes utilized for cargo transport. Likewise, India had a nonmotorized-vehicle area that included bullock trucks, bike rickshaws, horse-drawn carriages, and manual force trucks. The span of this nonmotorized fragment was huge yet undocumented.

Three Wheelers (auto rickshaws)

India was the world's largest three-wheeler market with 2005 sales of 307,887 units, representing a five-year compound yearly development rate of 14%. Three wheelers were utilized for the load (44% of offers) and traveler (56% of offers) development. These vehicles were prevalent in India because of their capacity to move through restricted roads and their low obtaining and working expenses. A run of the mill three wheelercostbetweenRs.100,000andRs.200,000($2,222–$4,444).Three wheelers were typically rated to convey heaps of 0.5 to 1.0 tons and were raise motor vehicles with 5– 10 pull, 1-barrel motors that kept running on fuel, diesel, or packed gaseous petrol (CNG). A three-wheeler could accomplish the best speed of 50 kilometers for every hour and mileage appraisals of 18 to 30 kilometers for each liter of diesel fuel.4Operating costs for a three-wheeler ran from Rs. 4 to Rs. 5 for each ton for every kilometer. Significant producers of three wheelers included Bajaj, Piaggio, Force Motors, and Mahindra &Mahindra.

Bajaj was the market pioneer in the three-wheeler section with a 51% piece of the pie. Bajaj offered diesel-, electric-, and CNG-fueled vehicles with 79% of its deals in the traveler fragment. Bajaj's vehicles were ordinarily utilized as a minimal effort Indian option in contrast to a taxi. Bajaj had lost a piece of the overall industry as of late because of Piaggio's more present day and bigger contributions. Starting in 2005, Bajaj produced three-wheelers, bikes, and cruisers.

Piaggio was an Italian organization that offered both travelers and load three wheelers in India. Piaggio had the capacity to build 150,000 vehicles in its plant in Maharashtra, India and used its Indian activities to trade items to Africa, Latin America, and Asia.5 Piaggio's The ape show, with a payload limit of 0.4 tons, had delighted in deals accomplishment because of its relative refinement contrasted with other Indian contenders and in light of the fact that it was the first to offer a diesel motor on an extensive scale. Starting in 2005, Piaggio had a piece of the overall industry of 26%.

Power Motors Formerly known as Bajaj Tempo, Force Motors offered three-wheelers, transports, business vehicles, and SUVs in the Indian market. Power's Minidor diesel three-wheeler was centered fundamentally around the payload portion with a 0.6 ton-appraised conveying limit. Power delighted in a dependable following in provincial markets, and its Minidor was the initial three-wheeler to offer a carlike guiding wheel when it was propelled in 1996.6Force Motors had a piece of the pie of8%.

Mahindra and Mahindra (M&M)M&M had its underlying foundations in building Jeeps, utility vehicles, and farm equipment in India. The company's products had a reputation for durability and had an broad deals and administration network.7M&M's three-wheeler contributions incorporated the Champion and Champion Alfa and were principally centered around load transport in the 0.5-to 0.65-to go. Starting at 2005, M&M had a piece of the pie of 7%.

Four Wheelers (LCVs)

In 2005, offers of four-wheeled light business vehicles (LCVs) (characterized as conveying 7.5 tons or less) were 119,877. The LCV portion included pulling trucks, pickups, and little transports. The LCV fragment was all the more firmly connected with the general financial atmosphere and had developed at a 22% compound yearly development rate from 2000 to 2005. Generally, the segment was additionally more patterned than the market for three wheelers or autos. LCVs were utilized for payload (83% of offers) and traveler (17% of sales)movement. LCV prices started at Rs.350,000($7,778) and were rated to carry loads of 1.2to7.5 tons. LCVs were regularly diesel-fueled vehicles with 60-to 100-torque motors. An LCV could accomplish the best speed of 100 kilometers for each hour and mileage evaluations of 9 to 10 kilometers for every liter of diesel fuel. Working expenses for an LCV went from Rs. 7 to Rs. 9 for every ton for each kilometer. Real members in the LCV section included Tata Motors, Mahindra and Mahindra, Swaraj Mazda, and Eicher Motors. Imported LCVs were phenomenal because of usefulness and durability concerns.

Goodbye Motors. Tata Motors was the market pioneer in the LCV portion, offering trucks with limits extending from 1.2 to 7 tons and also little transports. Starting in 2005, Tata Motors had a piece of the pie of 51%.

Mahindra and Mahindra (M&M)M&M offered the three-ton DI3200, which was a modernizedversionofaNissanvehiclefromthelate1980s.9 M&MalsoofferedtheTouristerlineof buses,whichseated11to26people,and pickup trucks that were based on its utility vehicles. As of 2005, M&M had a piece of the overall industry of33%.

Swaraj Mazda entered the Indian market in 1984 as a cooperation between Punjab Tractors and Mazda Motor Corporation of Japan.10The organization offered 3.5-to 7-ton trucks and transports all in view of a similar stage.

Starting at 2005, Swaraj Mazda had a piece of the pie of 5%.

Eicher Motors was shaped in 1982 and gone into a specialized coordinated effort with Mitsubishi Motors of Japan in 1986. The joint effort finished in 1994, after which Eicher started building up its own products.11Eicher offered trucks running from 3 to 25 tons and additionally transports. Eicher vehicles had a higher ground leeway, grade ability, and capacity to-weight proportion than those of the opposition. Starting in 2005, Eicher Motors had a piece of the overall industry of5%.

Truck drivers in India ordinarily overlooked payload evaluations and over-burden vehicles 30%– half over their appraised limit. Therefore, truck makers regularly centered around outlining solid items that could withstand the extra strain. Over-burdening regularly diminished vehicle quickening, mileage, and best speed, yet these contemplations were exceeded by the capacity to cut down the per unit cost of transport through huge burdens. Nonetheless, over-burdening designs were required to wind up more like those of global markets because of an Indian Supreme Court decided in November 2005 that prohibited over-burdening on roadways and called for weight checks and monetary punishments for resistance.

Street Transportation Infrastructure in India

By world norms, India's street arranges in 2006 was thought to be insufficient and immature. While India had 3.32 million kilometers of streets, just 2% were national thruways and just 12% of this 2% were four paths (two paths toward every path) or more.12Within urban territories, especially close business and retail showcases, streets were extremely tight and congested. Activity was additionally exacerbated by the absence of adherence to movement rules and the nearness of different vehicle composes people on foot, and creatures out and about. Street conditions frequently kept trucks from achieving retail markets, and last merchandise conveyance must be finished by means of three-wheelers, bullock trucks, or human work. These conveyance strategies frequently brought about harmed merchandise, longer lead times, and shrinkage.

Streets in rustic India were regularly inadequately cleared and needed markings. Rustic Indians needed to depend on these streets to transport their horticultural yield to urban zones. Cultivating was the predominant occupation in India, and it was directed in a profoundly divided way with every agriculturist freely owning and working a little plot. Subsequently, most ranchers were neither very much promoted nor did they require an expansive business vehicle to transport their collect.

The mantra

The mantra actually is very simple it is to reset rethink and reposition yourself or your brand to ensure that you get the best results even while you are not at your best. The actual fact is that once customers start recognizing your brand or start using your solution or service they tend to push your brand towards the tipping point that you could only have dreamt about in your wildest dream. This typing point will stay for As Long as you maintain the brand-customer centricity.

So what do you have to do to reach this tipping point? There are essentially 5 major steps which you need to keep repeating till the time your customer does not start recognizing your brand where ever and whichever format you might be available on any of the available mediums. The five factors which define the steps are as follows:

1. Analytics- analytics is the first factor which ensures that you understand and can relate easily with your customer by knowing when and what makes your customer respond, like, share, or comment on your post. The time when your customer is relax and on the medium of his or her choice is when the marketing manager must ensure that your post is there and also

showing exactly what the customer is looking for or is interested to know more about in the right format and also in the right medium which could be an image, video, text or plain music.

How to get another viewpoint on an old thought?

Not much, simply Rethink!

A youngster's interest and hunger for new learning frequently become mixed up in the progress to adulthood. This is particularly valid for grown-ups who have been in a similar profession for quite a while. Strength can transform into equality, and the unwavering quality can wind up unsurprising. You may get the incidental curveball tossed your direction, similar to some new date-book application or bookkeeping programming, yet that is about it.

Achievement today requires the dexterity and drive to reconsider, revitalize, respond and rehash continually. We have to re-examine the key premises of tutoring and choose what it is we need all kids to learn and why. We have to re-evaluate our situation on the planet and as an individual, what we ought to do to improve this world a place. It's an ideal opportunity to rest, re-evaluate and reposition.

Re-evaluating gives you consent to utilize your considerations to alter your opinion. Take what is and turn it around to give you another survey and a new point of view" – Susan C Young

As a tribute to each one of those re-thinkers, this year, the TEDx group picked the subject RETHINK. An Invite from their end is the thing that we are reaching out to our Hyderabad start up network in their very own words:

"Is it accurate to say that you are a supporter of an imaginative future or a survivor of history?

Do you have a neglected objective? Right now is an ideal opportunity to RETHINK your vision!

Have you lost a chance? Right now is an ideal opportunity to RETHINK your decisions!

Be it any field of work, how far would you say you will go and RETHINK?

Add to the future as we celebrate and salute uncommon RETHINK'ers

The need of the Hour? An intense chance yet a test? Why Change? What drives you to be the change. #RETHINK"

An extensive variety of speakers of novel foundations are as of now topping off the diagram, and we guarantee you that this year it will be huge and beyond anyone's imagination previously. So far we have,

Meghana, a worldwide honor winning Rhythmic Gymnast from India. Meghana was the main member from India for Rhythmic vaulting in the XXI Commonwealth Games 2018. She is very committed and prepares herself for almost 6 to 8 hours day by day, following her musical energy.

Harish Sadani, who runs an association called Men Against Violence and Abuse (MAVA).His one of a kind idea of bringing social equity of sex cleared roots to numerous inexplicable changes in the domain of women's liberation.

Sanjay Tumma, also called Vahchef, the renowned youtube star with a huge number of perspectives. He is additionally best culinary specialist regarded with numerous worldwide and national honors.

Vijay Chadda, who has 45+ years of expert involvement with 20 years, serving in the Indian Army. Under his initiative, the Satya Bharti School Program Bharti Foundation, gives free quality training to more than 45,000 kids from minimized networks in rustic zones, through its 254 schools crosswise over six Indian states.

Sandeep Sangaru, who is a multidisciplinary creator and business visionary. He won a few honors and honors, including the Red Dot Design Award in 2009 (thought to be the Oscar of item outline) and the British Council's Young Creative Entrepreneur Award – Design for Social Impact in 2012. He attempted to resuscitate the lost art of Pinjrakari and with Channapatna's wood-and-veneer craftsmen.

Colleen Lightbody, She is known as "The Brain Guru" through her composition for online journals and magazines, and additionally in TV and radio meetings.

Her specialized topic lies in Neuroscience, Mindfulness, Brain-based Learning, Personal and Professional Leadership, and Emotional Intelligence. Battling against claim shortcomings in her very own life made her the ace of care.

Anshul Sinha, He has partaken in excess of 500 film celebrations up until this point, winning in excess of 100 national and worldwide honors, and keeps on having an effect with his motion pictures. His most outstanding motion pictures are 'Passage to Heaven' on human body exchanging and 'Mitti – Back to roots' on agrarian emergency and agriculturist suicides.

Falguni Vasavada-Oza, A multidimensional Influencer, she holds a Ph.D. in Advertising and has been educating for two decades in the region of Marketing and Advertising. She is presently a Professor at MICA and cherishes to dissect how marks develop through the intensity of correspondence. Dr. Oza is a solid devotee to Gender Equality, Body Positivity, Women Empowerment, Work-Life Balance and Happiness as a Lifestyle and Motivation. She motivates to acknowledge one's body and dependable center around making a solid identity that goes past physical traits.

Giving up Can Be The Best Decision Ever

There's in no way like beginning once again.

Subsequent to experiencing my secondary school years, I discovered that a lesser year can be the season for significant changes. I came in about two months after what was a late spring of startling development that made me arranged for some substantial blows. Love has a method for telling you when it's a great opportunity to hang on and time to give up. At times, you need to surrender what you need to get what you require. I did and I have never felt so incredible.

My internal sanctum was diminished to the security of my four dividers put with purple; disengaged, by decision, in a pinnacle that happens to give a wide perspective of the outside world giving the chance to reset, reconsider, and reposition. INFJs are the loners who can act as an outgoing person yet at the same time require their alone time to revive. This must be what the best of the two universes is. Endless hours have been spent in my room however it is so justified, despite all the trouble having the capacity to stand tall alone when reality occurs, not having the dread of passing up a major opportunity take control of my activities until the end of time, and thumping outflanks solid.

Connections resemble glass; it's not worth wicked fingers to something that is past broken. That self-contradicting solace of realizing that you can give up and take the weight off your shoulders. Nobody individual in your life ought to characterize esteem, bliss. I feel that poisonous individuals are venturing squares who lead the individuals who draw out the best in us. When one entryway shuts, another entryway opens and this entryway came swinging completely open to where my grin is greater after in some way or another falling into this hover of common help and fondness that makes me feel stunning about myself.

I got the opportunity to experience that progress and it was just my fifth day back on grounds. I got the chance to encounter what genuine love gathered to be in a kinship in this present individual's absence. Tears were shed, components were changed, and I'll generally have the recollections however I'm discovering what I am really able to do. You never perceive how much nervousness, sorrow or torment you had in that materialistic thing, that propensity, or even that relationship/kinship that didn't work out until the point that you let go then go to the individual choice that you never need to be back in that place.

A few of us are clutching things from path back when and get befuddled regarding for what reason we're so on edge. It doesn't encourage you or anyone so why convey this dead weight? One is a forlorn number, it kinda makes you consider how beginning back at zero can feel so decent yet it feels perfect. When you understand that you merit better, giving up will be the best choice you've at any point made.

Google CFO Calls Glass A Case Where The Company Needed To "Pause" And "Reset"

Google's Chief Financial Officer Patrick Pichette wasn't too optimistic about the future of Google Glass on today's Google earnings call for Q4 2014. The executive took some time to highlight the project as an example of when Google is willing to take a step back and rethink something that isn't working out, even when they've made a considerable investment in the tech.

"When teams aren't able to [leap] hurdles, but we think there's still a lot of promise, we might ask them to take a pause and take the time to reset their strategy, as we recently did in the case of Glass," Pichette said. "[A]and in those situations where projects don't have the impact we hope for, we do take the tough calls, we make the decision to cancel them, and you've seen us do this time and time again."

Google discontinued the Glass Explorer program back on January 19, after announcing it would shut down and be reassigned to Tony Fadell's consumer hardware department within the company. Google is still encouraging developers to develop for the platform, and a repositioning under Fadell also doesn't indicate a finality of its fate, but Pichette's comments today are the most concrete statement we've heard on the Glass program's outcome from a top executive, and they certainly don't suggest an imminent consumer launch.

Glass might live on as something else, but Pichette's statements today suggest we might not recognize the form it takes when it does eventually re-emerge.

-https://techcrunch.com/2015/01/29/google-glass-patrick-pichette/

'WE F*CKED UP' ADMITS RBS GROUP CMO AS IT 'PRESSES RESET' ON NATWEST

RBS Group had to make a bold change in its marketing as the old way was 'fucking up' its brands, CMO David Wheldon says, as he launches an ambitious new strategy for NatWest that prioritizes taking accountability for its own actions, whether good or bad.

NatWest has propelled another TV advertisement, which previously circulated 23 September and has the trademark 'We are our main event', that implies real changes to the brand. It is a piece of another crusade that perceives banks ought to be in charge of what they do and in addition what they say, welcoming buyers to consider NatWest answerable for its activities.

The lead 60-second spot is both emotive and fair by rising to gauge, utilizing chronicle shots of British symbols, for example, Charlie Chaplin as a voiceover speaking to the NatWest mark says "we are overcome" and "we are creative".

Be that as it may, the advertisement additionally contains shots of football lawbreakers, as the voiceover includes "we are moronic" also.

Other 30-second variations, in the meantime, center around NatWest's objective to encourage a million youngsters about their funds by 2018 and how it has loaned more cash to homemakers than some other British bank.

In a straight to the point meet, the RBS Group's CMO David Wheldon disclosed to Marketing Week: "On account of Natwest, if a PC isn't working you hit the reset catch and that is the thing that we expected to do.

"This brand has been battered for quite a while and that is on the grounds that we overlooked where we originated from. At the point when NatWest began in 1968, the logo depended on the reality three banks met up for NatWest to exist and it was a 3D logo portraying that. It was about solidarity.

Read more: NatWest returns to its foundations with the new marking

"What our image chiefs had done was fuck that [branding] up by overlooking those thoughts even existed and supplanting the logo. We have needed to reconstruct the brand. What's more, that is the reason the 3D logo is presently back."

David Wheldon, CMO, RBS Group

Money related brands should be 'straightforward'

The most concerning issue, as indicated by Wheldon, has been the hesitance of monetary brands to be straightforward since the worldwide budgetary emergency developed in 2008. He currently needs NatWest's new marking to change all that.

"Throughout the most recent nine years, I can't think about a solitary monetary brand that has even gestured at the reality there were not kidding issues previously. It pesters individuals," he clarifies.

"We know we committed errors previously, yet we have gained from them and won't do them once more. In any case, we should recognize those errors and the 'we are our main event' motto truly outlines that."

What's more, in a wound at match Lloyds, he includes: "This isn't utilizing promotion dishonesty or iconography. See, it is flawless Lloyds has a dark steed logo and it goes moving over the scene. In any case, what does that need to do with what they do, all the live long day? Nothing.

"Indeed, the vast majority loathe banks, however, the greater part of our clients are likewise content with what we do. We needed to adjust those two things and grasp them."

More extensive changes

It has been a critical time of progress for the RBS Group. Recently, it reported a few brand changes, which were applauded by Marketing Week feature writer Mark Ritson.

NatWest

A still from the new NatWest battle

NatWest, which has held its personality in spite of huge back-of-house reconciliation into RBS, has turned into the gathering's real retail managing an account center for England and Wales; in Scotland, RBS has turned out to be Royal Bank of Scotland, and in England and Wales, in excess of 300 RBS branches are to be stripped from the organization.

Basically, RBS is resigning its job as a worldwide brand and centering the majority of its image endeavors on neighborhood markets.

Wheldon concedes the present vulnerability over Williams and Glyn, the name given to the piece of the organizations RBS is required to auction before the finish of 2017, is a "cerebral pain". Anyway, it is in "profound talk" with "various invested individuals" and he says there will be "some official news soon".

A reevaluate for Royal Bank of Scotland

NatWest isn't the only one in getting another battle, as Royal Bank of Scotland's most recent TV spot show on 26 September. Dissimilar to the new NatWest work, which was produced by M&C Saatchi, Wheldon entrusted the Scottish office, Leith, to administer the crusade.

The crusade takes after a Royal Bank of Scotland £10 note as it travels through the nation, going through the lives of Scotland's kin. Whedon trusts it demonstrates the brand has learned from its past slip-ups.

rbi

A still from the new Royal Bank of Scotland crusade

"On the off chance that you take a gander at our ongoing history, we have been committing an unpleasant error of doing likewise correspondence for the Royal Bank as we had for NatWest. The organization would complete a sprightly pleasant home loan advertisement for NatWest and in Scotland, it would be precisely the same, however with a Scottish voice and the RBS logo included toward the end. On the off chance that you were a Scottish client staring at the TV and after that you flipped over to Sky, we were demonstrating to you how little we thought about the brand," he concedes.

"I said to M&C Saatchi, you're not McSaatchi would you say you are? I needed to get to a Scottish office that truly got what the monetary order intends to Scots and for them to comprehend the neighborhood subtleties. Before it resembled the world was level to the RBS Group, however, we currently need to comprehend the neighborhood subtleties for every one of our brands."

Passing judgment on progress

So what will achievement resemble? Wheldon uncovers: "When I take a gander at the measurements we have, the stressing one is that brand attribution for NatWest publicizing was by and large at 56%. That implies we were squandering 44% of advertisement cash.

"When we had the end line 'accommodating keeping money', which was dropped four years back, the normal was 90%. That is the place we should be. Luckily, my directorate all back the new course we are setting out on and this is something we have worked from the back to front."

While the new NatWest and Royal Bank of Scotland battles will be conveyed through the standard social channels, for example, Facebook, Twitter, and Instagram, Wheldon isn't in a hurry to bounce onto new patterns, for example, 360 video or virtual reality.

"Once in a while advertisers rush to jump on the new sparkly thing without truly supposing it through. With the best will on the planet, does somebody need a 360-degree or VR experience of what it resembles to go to a NatWest money point? No. They simply need a bank that is straightforward and truly thinks about its clients.

"For a really long time at banks, promoting hasn't been considered important [by other departments] – it is that thing the odd individuals over yonder in the corner do. We need to change that for good."

You wouldn't wager against him.

-https://www.marketingweek.com/2016/09/24/we-fcked-up-admits-rbs-group-cmo-as-it-presses-reset-for-new-natwest-campaign/

MARKS & SPENCER'S RETAIL RETHINK

Neerja Sinha, 43, a senior official with a private bank, is an ongoing proselyte to the Marks and Spencer (M&S) outlet at Phoenix Mills, Central Mumbai's clamoring shopping center complex. Sinha, who has never been to an M&S store abroad, is currently dependent on it's not really bustling vibe and the particularly up showcase feel. She drops in at any rate once multi-month to purchase stuff worth a couple of thousand rupees for her home and children. "The store has truly turned out to be moderate over the most recent couple of months," she says.

Sinha is precisely the sort of client who will make Martin Jones, the new head of M&S' India activities, glad. In the course of the most recent 30 months, the specific British 9.5 billion pound shopping chain has been making a decent attempt to shed its selective and costly picture to make itself more open to Indian customers. Critically, in the following 30 months, it is clients like Sinha that M&S will endeavor to pull in to impel its eager development plan.

Early outcomes are encouraging. In spite of the fact that they won't talk particular numbers, a senior official says that a few stores' deals have expanded 25% since the choice to change was made. Fifteen months after the repositioning, M&S is reviving its development designs in the nation.

Jones needs to almost treble the number of stores to 50 from the present 18 by 2013. Store sizes are reliably expanding and M&S will now likewise be in littler and quickly developing urban areas the nation over. Despite the fact that M&S claims its Indian endeavor mutually with Reliance Retail, its extension here will be its boldest wager in any developing business sector. In China, another quickly developing business sector M&S straightforwardly put resources into, the organization is said to be as yet battling with the principal store that it built up a couple of years prior in Shanghai. "There is an awesome expectation in the central station that India may well be their greatest developing business sector achievement," says a senior M&S official, who did not wish to be named.

The purpose seems genuine up until this point. From 2000 till 2007, M&S in India was kept running as a franchisee task. Its neighborhood accomplice, Planet Retail, set up the stores and acquired stock from U.K. what's more, sold it here. M&S did not have any desire to change its capital in lieu of a cut in edges on the items it sold the franchise. It additionally permitted Planet Retail to have little stores of 5,000 to 8,000 square feet, contrasted with the worldwide standard of 15,000 square feet in addition to stores. This has changed in the new plan of things.

M&S went separate ways with Planet Retail - a franchisee who still runs its store in Indonesia - for the most part by virtue of the pace of development is needed in the nation. It was likewise dedicated to change the greatest barricade to its development in the nation - an observation that its stock was much excessively costly for its intended interest group. The brand was being seen as significantly more premium than it was in the U.K.

Jones' ancestor Mark Ashman, who was the main M&S leader of the Indian endeavor, immediately picked the low hanging organic product. Prior, M&S' franchisee imported garments from U.K., paid obligation and place them in the stores here. With import obligation at more than half, its garments appeared to be excessively expensive contrasted with the rivalry. Says Jones, "When we assumed control over the business we accepted a call to source more item from the South Asian locale. At the time pretty much a solitary digit level of items was privately sourced. Presently it is 42%. We expect to take it to 70% inevitable."

Ashman was likewise instrumental in rolling out minor improvements to stock to make it additionally speaking to the Indian client. M&S shirts donned a pocket out of the blue, and women shirts got longer. This was the first run through M&S confined its advertising. In light of the accomplishment of these tests, M&S is presently executing comparative changes in parts of Europe and China. "The precarious part was to demonstrate that clients loved what we did and this did not end up being a hazard to the brand," says an official, who was a piece of a group that purchased in the progressions.

There was additionally an inclination that M&S could have had a superior brand remaining than it as of now had. Benetton, which likewise began as a diversified activity, went free around a similar when M&S came to India. Benetton is presently viewed as more well known, as it had a more extended time to actualize its image procedure.

At the point when M&S went separate ways with Planet Retail, one purpose of contradiction was the measure of stores that were at that point in the nation. The franchise trusted that bigger stores in littler urban areas were unjustifiable, given the deals from existing stores. M&S officials felt that having littler stores would not give the expected involvement of the brand. In Mumbai, M&S multiplied the store measure, a feeling that customers like Sinha resound with now. Store sizes will be upwards of 15,000-25,000 square feet even in level II towns like Pune. In Amritsar, be that as it may, the organization has backpedaled on this procedure as it has opened a 7,000 square feet store as of late. "M&S should change even a portion of its center suggestions in the end," says an industry master.

In the U.K. what's more, even in China, M&S gets a considerable measure of incomes from sustenance and drinks, however, that line of business is as yet not practical in India. To develop the portfolio, M&S has presented two new lines of business: Home and children. In spite of the fact that deals from these lines are as yet inconsequential, and friends administrators say the two classifications have had soak expectations to absorb information, the organization is setting up sourcing connects to get less expensive items into the racks. The thought is to gradually bring the general M&S encounter into India as opposed to set incomes clicking immediately. Says Jones, "We are not attempting a manufacture a business just around clients who have been to M&S in the U.K. All that we are doing with item recommendation, client experience, and store configuration is gone for focusing on the mid-market Indian shopper in a way that is important and engaging them."

Will M&S' recently discovered intensity ensure a beneficial business in the following five years? Specialists feel that it might be too early to give an answer. As of now, their development designs have been hampered by delays in store opening. Contenders like Esprit are taking in the business rapidly. Esprit purchased down the retail cost of its cotton shirts specifically sourced from Vietnam by Rs. 1,000 in the course of the most recent one year. It is additionally setting up a nearby sourcing instrument. Jack and Jones, the prevalent European sportive brand, has additionally started bringing privately sourced items. The key, thusly, will lie in situating its image solidly in the Indian client's mind.

Devangshu Dutta, CEO, retail consultancy Third Eyesight says, "In the U.K., they are solid amidst the market. Their new technique to have more mass stock in India ought not to adjust that."

- https://www.forbes.com/2010/10/05/forbes-india-marks-and-spencer-repositioning-in-india.html#6b1d3a0e6de3

How to find whether or not to use or not use the mantra? What are the factors and what to look out for?

If you have been able to link Google Analytics with your website then that could prove to be a very rich and early indicator of what is needed or looked at by the customers. Google analytics can give you an in-depth and detailed interests of your visiting customers and also can help you better understand their interest regions.

What and why Google Analytics?

Google analytics in a way tracks all of your users who are visiting your site and also understands their behavior and likes & dislikes by almost following them to all the sites that they visit before your site and even after they have moved out of your site. Google Analytics also tags and views their behavior even while they are within the boundaries of your site, it means that it understands which page or section is the user currently on and for how long has the user being on the same page. Google analytics could be a very rich point of gaining customer information for free. Imagine if you are in the niche market and have a very specific product line which is targeted towards the 60+ Then one visit to Google analytics -> User demographics can tell you if your targeting or keywords are right or wrong. Or if you are in the business of selling exquisites then if your target market is not the one coming to your site then there is something absolutely wrong with the way you are marketing or your sales guys are targeting as this is as clear as it can ever be like. Google analytics acts as a mirror for you. It will only show you who you want to be for your customer or what your customer thinks you are with of course areas where you can improve to get better.

So Google Analytics is not a death sentence but it surely is a free tool which can help you go a long way but for this to happen you may need to focus on understanding it better and start taking its tips. Google Analytics is like your trident but if you don't know how to use it or don't understand why you may need to indulge your time to understand it, it could also prove to become your biggest foe as it keeps screaming out your best customers views without any filters but in the way of numbers. Google analytics is the straightforward sales sheet for every businessman which tells you how much is your business worth and how long is it going to survive without your best salesman or person.

Google analytics now can also give you an in-depth into the likes and dislikes of your audience. Google Analytics 5 took the best highlights of their examination program and made it much simpler to use with the new association and perception highlights. Here are nine great things you can do with Google Analytics 5 that will enable you to capitalize on your investigation data and utilize it to enhance your site's substance, changes, and client encounter.

1. See your most vital examination information first.

On the off chance that there are (at least one) bits of information you need to see initially every time you log in to your examination, make certain to set it up in the Dashboards region.

You can make numerous dashboards, every one of which can contain various gadgets. To make another dashboard, essentially go under Dashboards in the menu bar of your investigation and after that select New Dashboard. At that point include your gadgets. You can browse gadgets that show you one specific metric, a pie outline contrasting measurements, a course of events of one to two measurements, or a table demonstrating a measurement with two particular measurements. Each sort of gadget can likewise be separated.

The best piece of the dashboards is you can change the date range and see the majority of your gadgets refresh with that date range's information. This is incredible on the off chance that you need to see an outline of your details for activity, objective fruitions, and different measurements of your picking across the board put.

2. Discover which online crusades bring the most activity and transformations.

Have you been interested which of your web-based showcasing efforts (anything from nearby hunt to internet-based life promoting) are the best as far as conveying movement and transformations to your site? At that point, it's a great opportunity to take a gander at your propelled portions.

To make a propelled fragment, tap on the Advanced Segments dropdown and after that the New Custom Segment. In the event that you needed to track movement from nearby inquiry indexes, at that point call your custom fragment Local Search Profiles and begin entering the destinations you have profiles on, for example, maps.google.com/maps/for Google Places and yelp.com for your Yelp posting.

When you have entered the majority of the areas you need to track, you can see the fragment to guarantee it is pulling the correct information and after that spare the portion. To see it, tap on the Advanced Segments, check the custom section you need to view and snap apply. Presently you can see the majority of your activity and objective change information that touches base from those sources which will give you a smart thought of what is working the best for your site. With the correct custom sections, you can discover the ROI of your internet based life battle and additionally your other web-based promoting techniques.

3. Figure out where your best guests are found.

Have you considered utilizing publicizing through Google, Facebook, StumbleUpon, or different administrations? If not, it may be an overwhelming undertaking to figure out who you should focus amid your advertisement setups. A considerable lot of them will inquire as to whether you need to center around a particular nation or focus on your advertisement around the world.

Because of Google Analytics, you don't have fuss anymore. Just look under your Visitors menu to see the Location socioeconomics of your guests.

Here, you can see your overall details, including the normal time nearby and bob rate of guests from specific nations. You can likewise bore down to specific nations and see these details and also your objective change rates specifically areas.

Presently you will know the particular areas whose guests present to you the most transformations. Focusing on guests in these areas with your promotions will result in considerably more objective culminations for your site.

4. Realize what individuals are hunting down on your site.

The vast majority know how to discover the catchphrases that convey guests to their locales from web indexes. In any case, how might you want to go past that to discover what guests are looking once they are on your site?

In the event that your site has an inquiry box, simply ahead and play out a pursuit to see the URL of the query items. When you have this for your site, tap on the settings wheel symbol in the upper right corner of your Analytics menu bar and discover your Profile Settings. Under Site Search Settings, select the alternative to Do track Site Search and enter s as the inquiry parameter (or the one that accommodates your site's URL structure).

To see the aftereffects of this setup, go to the Content menu and the Site Search region. Under Usage, you can perceive what terms are being scanned for, if guests refined their pursuit, kept perusing your site, or left which will fill you in as to whether they are finding what they need. Under Pages, you can see which pages individuals are upon when they choose to utilize the hunt highlight. When you tap on each page, you can perceive what terms they hunt down.

Site Search can enable you to decide whether individuals are finding what they are searching for on your site. It can likewise give you thoughts of which pages of your substance require more particular data and also the new substance you can make on your site to additionally connect with your guests.

5. Imagine what individuals tap on the most.

Inquisitive where individuals are making the most taps on your site? In-Page Analytics under the Content menu will pull up your site in the Analytics program with data on the level of snaps that have occurred on each inside connection on your site.

You can drift over each connects to see extra points of interest and navigate to more pages on your site to see more subtle elements. This can help you outwardly observe what zones of your site are the most prominent, and help you recognize where individuals are tapping on your site. So on the off chance that you have a specific connection, you need guests to see, you ought to make sure to put it in the zones of your site that get the most snaps.

6. Reveal your best substance.

Need to know which pages keep your guests on your site the longest, or have the most reduced bob rate? You can see this rapidly by going under the Content menu and choosing Pages under Site Content.

This segment can enable you to distinguish which bits of substance keep guests on your site the longest and prompt them needing to proceed onto more pages on your site. This can enable you to create more substance that individuals will like later on.

7. Distinguish your most exceedingly bad performing pages.

A couple of things down in the substance menu from your best pages are your best leave pages. This will reveal to you what number of individuals are arriving and leaving on a specific page.

This is to some degree basic for web journals as individuals are coming to locate a specific snippet of data and afterward leave (ideally) fulfilled. Be that as it may, for different sites, it might mean that individuals are not finding what they are searching for on that page and after that clearing out. This may imply that you have to assess your site's substance to guarantee that guests are finding what they need and getting a suggestion to take action so they get where you need them to be before they leave, for example, buying into a mailing rundown or buying an item.

8. Figure out where individuals desert the shopping basket.

Does your site have a different advance checkout process? Assuming this is the case, you should set up an objective for your site utilizing a Goal Funnel. To do as such, tap on the settings wheel symbol and tap on Goals. Make another objective with the Goal Type of URL Destination. After you enter the fundamental objective points of interest, including the last URL of the checkout procedure (normally a thank you for your request page), at that point check the Use pipe box to enter every one of the URLs that compare to the means a guest must take when acquiring a thing.

By utilizing this setup, you will then have the capacity to see reports demonstrating to you when individuals surrender their shopping basket amid their buying procedure.

On the off chance that you take note of an especially high measure of individuals who exit on the installment page, you'll realize that you have to do some work with a specific end goal to make that page additionally shopping benevolent. Or on the other hand if individuals exit before affirming their request, you'll realize that there is something missing that is making individuals not have any desire to click that last catch. Settling these issues can prompt more deals over the long haul!

9. Find in the event that you require a portable site.

Have you been thinking about whether you require a versatile form of your site? Discover by looking under the Visitors menu. There you will locate a Mobile choice where you can see the distance down to a particular gadget and the level of your aggregate visits that are from a cell phone.

The key on this screen is taking a gander at the normal time nearby and the ricochet rate. On the off chance that your normal time nearby is lower and the skip rate is higher than your general numbers, at that point you'll realize that you're losing that a lot of your versatile activity.

What is the Google Webmaster tool?

Google Webmaster Tools is a free administration that encourages you to to assess and keep up your site's execution in query items (1). Offered as a free support of any individual who claims a site, Google Webmaster Tools (GWT) is a channel of data from the biggest web index on the planet to you, offering bits of knowledge into how it sees your site and helping you reveal issues that need settling.

You don't have to utilize GWT for your site to show up in query items, however, it can offer you significant data that can help with your advertising endeavors.

How GWT can help screen your site's execution

1. It checks that Google can get to the substance on your site.

2. GWT makes it conceivable to submit new pages and presents for Google on slithering and evacuate content you don't need internet searcher clients to find.

3. It encourages you to to convey and assess content that offers clients a more visual affair.

4. You can keep up your site without disturbing its essence in indexed lists.

5. It enables you to find and take out malware or spam issues that may not be effectively found through different means.

How GWT causes you to see how Google look sees your site

1. It reveals to you the most prominent questions making your site show up in indexed lists.

2. It reveals to you which inquiries are driving the most activity.

3. You can see which sites are connecting to yours.

4. You can assess how well your portable site is performing for individuals looking on tablets and telephones.

The most effective method to set up GWT

Prior to getting to any information, you need to check that you are the proprietor, or approved delegate, of the site. There are five different ways you can check your site. One isn't generally superior to the next, so you can pick which choice is the most straightforward for you (2).

Transferring an HTML record - Google gives you a document with a particular name that you need to transfer to the root registry of your site. The document itself is clear. Its solitary reason for existing is to help demonstrate that you approach the site's FTP server and can drop documents where they have to go. Once the record goes into the root catalog, simply tap on the "check" catch in GWT, and you will approach information.

Including an HTML tag - You can likewise confirm the site by including a meta tag given by Google that you can drop into the header of your landing page. When this is set up, tap on the "check" catch to see the information. It's imperative to take note of that occasionally landing page code can be trying to discover with certain substance administration framework (CMS) subjects, especially WordPress. It is additionally conceivable that your code may vanish when you refresh your landing page, denying your entrance to GWT information until the point that the tag is supplanted.

Select the supplier of your area - Google gives you the choice of choosing your space name supplier in a drop-down rundown. Tap on your supplier, and Google will walk you through the means of confirming your site.

Utilize Google Analytics - As the manager of your site's Google Analytics account, you can check the site utilizing nonconcurrent following code put in the leader of your landing page.

Utilizing Google Tag Manager - this is a device that enables you to enter and deal with all the following labels for your site, including GWT.

Once your record is set up and your site is confirmed, you will approach a lot of noteworthy information that can enable you to enhance your site. You can get alarms from Google, alter settings to convey particular data to your inbox, submit XML webpage maps and view client inquiries where your site showed up in the hunt. Take in the nuts and bolts of utilizing GWT, and you will have an extraordinary asset on which to base your future promoting choices.

What & why to use Google Seach Console?

Google Search Console is a free administration offered by Google that encourages your screen and keep up your site's essence in Google Search results. You don't need to agree to accept Search Console for your site to be incorporated into Google's indexed lists, however, doing as such can enable you to see how Google sees your site and advance its execution in query items.

Why utilize the Search Console?

Screen your site's execution in Google Search results:

Ensure that Google can get to your substance

Submit new substance for creeping and expel content you don't need to be appeared in indexed lists

Make and screen content that conveys outwardly captivating indexed lists

Keep up your site with negligible interruption to seek execution

Screen and resolve malware or spam issues so your site remains clean

Find how Google Search—and the world— see your site:

Which inquiries made your site show up in list items?

Did a few inquiries result in more rush hour gridlock to your site than others?

Are your item costs, organization contact information, or occasions featured in rich indexed lists?

Which destinations are connecting to your site?

Is your portable site performing admirably for guests looking on versatile?

Who should utilize Search Console?

Anybody with a site! From generalist to master, from amateur to cutting edge, Search Console can encourage you.

An entrepreneur who delegates. Regardless of whether you don't think you know how to utilize Search Console, you ought to know about it and get comfortable with the rudiments. You may employ your website admin or an advertising pro to enable you to set up your site with Search Console. All things considered, you can work with that individual to guarantee you approach and control to the majority of the reports for your site. Moreover, it's a smart thought to take in everything you can about how your site is performing in indexed lists so you can settle on essential business choices about your site.

Website design enhancement expert or advertiser. As somebody concentrated on web-based showcasing,

Search Console will enable you to screen your site movement, advance your positioning, and settle on educated choices about the presence of your website's indexed lists. You can utilize the data in Search Console to impact specialized choices for the site and do advanced showcasing examination related to other Google instruments like Analytics, Google Trends, and Google Ads.

Site Administrator. As a site administrator, you care about the solid activity of your site. Pursuit Console lets you effectively screen and sometimes settle server mistakes, site stack issues, and security issues like hacking and malware. You can likewise utilize it to guarantee any site support or alterations you make happen easily as for pursuit execution.

Web Developer. In the event that you are making the genuine markup and additionally code for your site, Search Console causes you screen and resolve basic issues with markup, for example, blunders in organized information.

Application Developer. On the off chance that you claim an application, you need to perceive how portable clients discover your application utilizing Google Search. Pursuit Console can enable you to incorporate your application flawlessly with the site world.

What & why to use Google Trends?

Google Trends is a pursuit patterns highlight that shows how every now and again a given inquiry term is gone into Google's web crawler with respect to the webpage's aggregate hunt volume over a given timeframe. Google Trends can be utilized for relative catchphrase examine and to find occasion activated spikes in watchword look volume.

Google Trends gives catchphrase related information including seeking volume file and topographical data about internet searcher clients.

Instructions to Use Google Trends

You can investigate Google Trends starting from the top by visiting the instrument and seeing what seeks are at present drifting, at that point delving into a theme for more data. For instance, Google Trends as of late shared data on inclining seeks identified with Hurricane Irma, for example, top important hunt terms over the U.S. Furthermore, top "how to" seek questions in Florida.

what is google patterns

You can likewise enter an inquiry term into the pursuit box at the highest point of the apparatus to perceive how look volume has fluctuated for that term after some time and in various areas. Change the area, time span, classification or industry, and sort of pursuit (web, news, shopping, or YouTube) for all the more fine-grained information.

utilizing google patterns

In the U.S., looks for "mulch" crest in April

This information can be exceptionally helpful for advertisers. For instance, on the off chance that you maintain a regular business, (for example, a home and planting supply store), you'll need to increase your advertising endeavors when look terms important to your business are inclining. Amid spikes in inquiry volume, your expense per click in AdWords will probably be higher, so make sure to assign more spending plan for your AdWords spend when your items or administrations are drifting.

To look at different terms, utilize the "+ Add examination" include:

google patterns tips

From this diagram, we can see "lead age" is around 7 times more famous than "request age" in web seek

Google Trends likewise indicates you related hunt terms and how to seek intrigue differs by subregion:

google patterns information

You can utilize the information found in Google Trends for a few diverse advertising purposes:

In the paid inquiry, Google Trends information can be utilized to educate your regular battles, assisting with cost arranging and stock stocking. Moreover, you can utilize Google Trends to discover unimportant slanting terms you have to set as negative catchphrases, so a drifting hunt doesn't uncontrollably influence your expenses.

For SEO and substance showcasing, utilize Google Trends to realize what individuals in your objective market are scanning for data about. Expounding on drifting subjects can enable drivers to activity to your site.

To move your advertisement innovative, peruse Google Trends to perceive what subjects are right now catching general society creative ability. Referencing a slanting theme (like a hot new sort of music or move) in your promoting efforts, regardless of whether it's an email impact, a Facebook advertisement, or a radio spot can build your promotions' commitment.

Why & What is Google Surveys?

Google Surveys 360: The Digital Marketer's New Best Friend

The Google Analytics 360 Suite offers a groundbreaking and incorporated examination answer for organizations everything being equal. The devices enable advertisers to gauge and enhance the effect of their promoting over each screen, direct and minute in the present client venture.

Since the dispatch in 2012 of Google Consumer Surveys, the offering has kept on developing in both extension and core interest. The center Google Consumer Surveys item gives clients a less expensive, quicker approach to review an agent test of their objective online populace over the web and on cell phones. In only 2016 alone a huge number of organizations have directed a huge number of meetings utilizing GCS, educating huge scale look into activities and affecting business choices around the globe. GCS approaches more than 10M+ accessible respondents through accomplice distributer destinations and 5M+ downloads on the versatile application, Google Opinion

Rewards, making a special example wellspring of genuine, ordinary individuals.

By all measures, GCS has been a fruitful item and it has quickened the DIY and computerization drifts in statistical surveying.

Being Google, obviously, one of the primary zones of the center for the organization has been utilizing cases identified with promoting examination and incorporation with the numerous other information investigation apparatuses Google offers. I most definitely have been sitting tight for a long while to perceive how (or if!) the combination into the more extensive Google Analytics stage would occur, however, the hold up is finished: Google Surveys is presently Google Surveys 360 and is a piece of the more extensive Google Analytics 360 suite.

The Google Analytics 360 Suite offers a ground-breaking and incorporated investigation answer for organizations all things considered. The instruments enable advertisers to gauge and enhance the effect of their showcasing over each screen, direct and minute in the present client venture. It's anything but difficult to utilize, makes information open for everybody, and enables clients to find and initiate the "has" they have to win. Here is more from their site:

With its forefront innovation, the Analytics 360 Suite forms huge measures of complex data—then streamlines it all—so your undertaking can without much of a stretch spot experiences and put them instantly to utilize. It gives one client encounter a solitary login and it's completely stacked with cross-item information reconciliations.

Stacked with six different items, four of which are fresh out of the box new and in beta, the Google Analytics 360 Suite makes it simple to share information and bits of knowledge all through your association.

The full suite incorporates:

Gathering of people Center 360, another information administration stage that gives you an all-encompassing perspective of the groups of onlookers that issue most to your image. Locally coordinated with DoubleClick, it consequently offers access to Google restrictive information and outsider information.

Enhance 360, another site testing and personalization device. Demonstrate your client's distinctive varieties of your site, at that point utilize and refine the best-performing alternatives to expand client commitment with your image.

Information Studio 360, our new information representation instrument, do the math and transforms them into flawlessly useful reports: simple to peruse, simple to share, and completely adaptable so your groups can get precisely what they require.

Label Manager 360 is new and composed only for big business with Google's industry driving label administration innovation. It offers improved information gathering and great APIs for better information precision and streamlined work processes.

Investigation 360, in the past known as GA Premium, combines information about client conduct into a solitary item and makes it simple to perform the vigorous examination. Get noteworthy client bits of knowledge and after that utilization those bits of knowledge to acquire more from your promoting.

Attribution 360, some time ago known as Adometry, enables promoters to see the estimation of their media ventures and assign spending plans with certainty. Presently modified starting from the earliest stage, it causes you to to break down execution over all channels and gadgets to accomplish the most intense showcasing blend.

Overviews 360, previously Google Consumer Surveys, allows advertisers lead great, modest and effective reviews from a worldwide example, or study site guests through re-focusing on or the advancement of altered boards and profound conduct focusing on. Improved expository instruments like cross arrangements take into account investigation of the information or joining with information from different apparatuses in the 360 suite.

The Google Analytics 360 Suite coordinates with other Google arrangements like AdWords, the Google Display Network and Google BigQuery. Match it with DoubleClick Bid Manager to achieve your best clients at the correct minutes with the auto-streamlined offering. Utilize your site information to portion high-esteem clients and remarket to them consequently. This is genuinely close to home and ongoing publicizing — at scale.

As a feature of the new coordination, the Google Surveys 360 UI was revamped starting from the earliest stage to be basic and simple to use, with new intelligent crosstabs.

The new Google Surveys 360 is situated as an undertaking stage and has another valuing model associated with it in view of a yearly membership in addition to per utilize charges, however for the individuals who have been utilizing Google Consumer Surveys no stresses: the compensation as-you-go arrangement will even now be accessible for the individuals who don't require propelled highlights and support.

The enormous news here other than the fuse of dynamic overviews device into the 360 suite is the thing that that implies for advertisers, particularly to target. Utilize the unrivaled information that Google has and bits of knowledge into who is visiting most any site on the planet, you can now retarget individuals who have visited your site, saw your recordings, tapped on your connections, and so on… Think about the conceivable outcomes for coordinated and iterative testing of promotions, ideas, content, and so on… with individuals you know are your intended interest group! Presently as opposed to simply having engaging insights from the conventional Google Analytics apparatuses, computerized advertisers and scientists would now be able to get to the "why" by means of overview capacities, adding monstrous profundity to web investigation, and utilizing web examination to add gigantic profundity to reviews.

Furthermore, with their open API, advertisers and specialists can build up a large group of new arrangements "fueled by" Google Surveys 360 to broaden the usefulness and utilize instances of the center stage in new ways.

In view of my discussions with advertisers and computerized information researchers and the battles they confront day by day, I speculate that with this new offering Google Surveys 360 may turn into the new BFF of Digital Marketers. Here is a case of how they incorporated different instruments in the 360 suite:

Utilizing Google Surveys 360 and Google Attribution 360 together, we could rapidly answer inquiries around TV advertisement execution amid the Rio 2016 Olympics. We at that point showed this information utilizing Google Data Studio (beta).

The dividers among research and promoting have been descending for some time, yet with Google Surveys 360 we are at long last taking a gander at a coordinated arrangement that consolidates a portion of the best of advanced examination with statistical surveying abilities in a simple to utilize yet intense stage. The open doors for advertisers to settle on better choices from better date are monstrous. I said in 2012 that Google was "in it to win it", and they have kept on ended up being valid with the dispatch of Google Surveys 360.

What is Google Content Experiments and why use it?

Content Experiments has three fundamental territories: the analysis setup wizard, the rundown of tests, and the individual reports for each trial. What's more, you can likewise observe information about your analysis in your Analytics see.

Examination Wizard

On the off chance that you have not made any tests, when you open Content Experiments, you see the diagram page for the test setup wizard. To make an analysis from this page, click START EXPERIMENTING.

On the off chance that you have just made different analyses, when you open Content Experiments, you see the trials list.

To make an investigation from this page, click Create test.

Regardless of whether you begin from the review page or from the investigation list, the setup-wizard opens so you can finish four stages:

Pick the goal of your test

Select the object for which you need to enhance transformations or the metric for which you need to enhance execution, and the level of activity you need to incorporate.

Distinguish the first and variety pages

Enter the URLs for the first page you need to test and for up to 10 varieties of that page.

Add the trial code to your unique page

While a lot of an investigation utilizes your Analytics following code, you have to add the trial code to one page. In case you're not happy with working with page code and you have somebody who can enable you, To content Experiments can send an email to ask for assistance from that individual.

When you click Next Step, Experiments checks to ensure your unique and variety pages are working appropriately.

Survey and dispatch your analysis

Now, audit your setup, at that point begin your investigation.

Content Experiments consequently spares all the data you enter amid setup so you can stop and resume anytime. To continue setting up a test, open the rundown and tap the investigation name.

Test list

After you make your first analysis, the examination list is the principal page you see when you open Content Experiments and gives a speedy review of every one of your trials.

Open the trial rundown to see:

Critical warnings about your trials

Which tests are running

Regardless of whether an examination created a triumphant page

What date the examination began

What date the investigation finished

You can make new investigations from this page, and also look through your current trials.

Examination report

When you click an analysis in the rundown, a definite report for that test opens.

Data in the report incorporates:

The status of your trial

How the pages in your trial are performing

Regardless of whether a specific page is unmistakably beating the rest

You can likewise take activities on analyses, including:

Ceasing a trial

Changing the level of your site's clients who see the trial

Changing who gets advised by email about changes to an analysis

Impairing a specific page

Benefits of using Google Content Experiments:

In the event that you have a site, you have exercises that you need your clients to finish (e.g., make a buy, agree to accept a pamphlet) as well as measurements that you need to enhance (e.g., income, session length, ricochet rate). With Content Experiments, you can test which adaptation of a greeting page results in the best change in transformations (i.e. finished exercises that you measure as objectives) or metric esteem. You can test up to 10 varieties of a point of arrival.

On the off chance that you need to direct tries different things with your applications, you can utilize the Experiments API, or you can make those examinations in Tag Manager. You can likewise utilize the API for website page tests.

Content Experiments utilizes a to some degree unexpected methodology in comparison to standard A/B and multivariate testing. Content Experiments utilizes an A/B/N display. You're not trying only two adaptations of a page as in A/B testing, and you're not trying different mixes of parts on a solitary page as in multivariate testing. Rather, you are trying up to 10 full forms of a solitary page, each conveyed to clients from a different URL.

What you can do with Content Experiments in Analytics

With Content Experiments, you can:

Look at how changed site pages or application screens perform utilizing an irregular example of your clients

Characterize what level of your clients are incorporated into the test

Pick which target you'd get a kick out of the chance to test

Get refreshes by email about how your trial is getting along

A case of utilizing examinations to enhance your business

Suppose you have a site where you offer housekeeping administrations. You offer essential cleaning, profound cleaning, and nitty-gritty cleaning. Point by point cleaning is most painful of the three, so you're keen on getting more individuals to buy this choice.

Most clients arrive on your landing page, so this is the principal page that you need to use for testing. For your test, you make a few new forms of this page: one with a major red feature for nitty gritty cleaning, one in which you develop the advantages of point by point cleaning, and one where you put a symbol by the connection to buy definite cleaning.

Once you've set up and propelled your test, an arbitrary example of your clients see the distinctive pages, including your unique landing page, and you essentially hold up to see which page gets the most elevated level of clients to buy the itemized cleaning.

When you see which page drives the most transformations, you can make that one the live page for all clients and rest assured that the transformations will continue as it is a tested & proven stuff.

Some gurus to follow in the year 2018

The intensity of learning can't be characterized by anybody. The best thing about being in any business is that you have a few models set in that very field that you can pursue and gain from. Regardless of which business or industry you have a place with, you can likewise end up effective. The main thing that you will require, aside from diligent work and commitment, will think about the fruitful individuals in the business that you are a piece of.

On the off chance that you have a place with the computerized advertising Agency and have been searching for how to end up an advanced advertiser and lift your business, at that point the rundown that we have aggregated down underneath will be a treat for you.

For turning into the best player in this exceedingly focused field of advanced showcasing, you should gain from the best computerized promoting masters. You should ponder how they function and should pursue their 'voyage to accomplishment's in full detail keeping in mind the end goal to distinguish the means that you can use in your profession and turn things to support you.

We concocted assembling a rundown of the main 10 advanced promoting masters keeping in mind the end goal to enable individuals to gain from them and copy their achievement in your own vocations. We should examine the rundown of the main 10 computerized showcasing masters!

Seth Godin

On the off chance that you have a place with the advanced media promoting industry and you haven't heard the name of Seth Godin, at that point trust us – you have not investigated the computerized showcasing field enough. Seth Godin is an internet advertising master and truly, is one of the main players in this field.

Best of all, aside from being a well-known advertiser and blogger, he has additionally thought of probably the most mainstream showcasing books, for example, All advertisers are liars, Tribes, Purple Cow, Linchpin, and so forth. Seth Godin has composed 18 books on showcasing to date, and not surprisingly, a large portion of them have gathered goliath prominence and can without much of a stretch be classified under top rated advertising books accessible in the market.

His books have been converted into almost thirty-five dialects. His websites are perused by a great many individuals around the world. His articles are not long, but rather they have the ability to accumulate a great many retweets inside a matter of few days.

Neil Patel

Neil Patel isn't only a web-based promoting master; he is an effective business visionary, SEO master, blogger, and a holy messenger financial specialist. Neil Patel is additionally the prime supporter of million-dollar organizations, for example, Crazy Egg, Quick Sprout, and KISSmetrics.

He has additionally helped a portion of the prominent organizations, for example, NBC, HP, Viacom, Amazon, and GM to develop their incomes. Neil Patel as of late propelled his blog NeilPatel.com. On Neil

Patel's blog, you can discover tips and thoughts that one can use for bringing 100,000 guests consistently.

His composing mostly centers around themes, for example, SEO, building your image name in the online world, and promoting. You will be astounded to realize that Neil Patel has assembled two multimillion online organizations and he is only 30 years of age.

Brian Clark

Brian Clark had an exceptionally unobtrusive begin. He began by being a performance blogger, and with time, he refined his composition craftsmanship and utilized the accessible assets to fabricate a multimillion-dollar online business. In all actuality, the thing that he did with his profession as an essayist isn't a simple errand to imitate. In all actuality, he is a genuine substance essayist, marketing specialist, and his substance can offer itself.

He assembled his gathering of people sans preparation. He began his adventure back in the year 2006. With his composition aptitudes, he has taken blogging to an unheard of level. He shows individuals how they can construct steadfast gatherings of people or perusers who are additionally potential clients.

His first online course "Showing Sells" was a hit as he made his current Copyblogger perusers figure out how they can construct gainful sites. The specific first course that he propelled was a hit. From that point onward, he propelled a couple of more courses on the web and subsequently, the gigantically effective Studiopress Company.

Fellow Kawasaki

In the event that you are searching for an online senior showcasing master whose life voyage and achievements can train you how to impersonate his accomplishment in your own vocation, at that point we would propose you pursue Guy Kawasaki sincerely.

At the beginning of his profession, he was an Apple representative working in the Macintosh division (when Apple was propelled) and is as of now a Silicon Valley advertising official. He is additionally the writer of the absolute most famous showcasing books accessible available.

A portion of the well-known books of Guy Kawasaki is "The craft of online life," "The specialty of the begin" and a couple of different books. Fellow Kawasaki holds an MBA from UCLA and has gotten a privileged doctorate from Babson College and BA from Stanford University. You will be shocked to realize that Guy Kawasaki is the brand envoy of Mercedes Benz in the USA.

Ramit Seth

Ramit Seth hails from India and is at present settled in the US. He is a blogger, and he runs a website identified with fund named "I Will Teach You to Be Rich." The best part about this webpage is that it has a large number of perusers from everywhere throughout the world. Ramit Seth is additionally the writer of a book with indistinguishable title and name from the blog.

His book turned into the New York Times Bestselling book. His fund lessons have been secured by a portion of the greatest magazines, for example, Forbes, Fortune Inc., and a couple of different magazines. He makes a decent measure of cash by offering on the web items that are costly.

Darren Rowse

Darren Rowse is an open speaker, full-time blogger, and blog advisor. You will be amazed to realize that he is additionally the originator of probably the most famous websites and blog systems, for example, ProBlogger, advanced photography-school.com, and b5media. As it were, he is a standout amongst the most experienced bloggers on this very rundown.

He began blogging while "blogging" was a straightforward word, and not very many knew about its criticalness and significance. Computerized Photography School blog is where he applies and checks the ongoing blogging tips in which he accepts and those he shares at ProBlogger.

Various individuals have this regular misguided judgment that an enormous piece of his procuring originates from ProBlogger. Be that as it may, in actuality, it's not valid as the lion's share of Darren's pay originates from Digital Photography School. This very site has a great many perusers and notwithstanding that, has an equivalent number of email endorsers. His a great many perusers are constantly anxious to purchase the cameras and DSLRs that Darren Rowse suggests.

Zac Johnson

Zac Johnson is a notable name in the internet showcasing industry as he is a standout amongst the most famous six-figures-procuring advanced promoting experts who has 20 years of involvement in his pack. He gains a large number of dollars consistently essentially by offering items on the web.

Simply envision how well he has manufactured his notoriety among his perusers and situated himself in the consistently changing web-based advertising world as an offshoot advertiser and one of the best web advertisers on the planet. He has established effective showcasing websites like ZacJohnson.com and Blogging Tips.

A huge number of individuals from a various piece of the world read his blog and indiscriminately acknowledge his recommendations. The best thing about Zac Johnson is that he truly instructs his perusers and aides them to purchase the correct items.

Jay Baer

Jay Baer is a well known American showcasing specialist, a broadly popular promoting blogger, writer of one of the NYT smash hit book titled "Youtility" and an open speaker. On the off chance that you wish to pick up accomplishment in your profession and gain ubiquity that can influence your blog to create a decent measure of cash for you, at that point you ought to clearly pursue Jay Bare's vocation.

Jay Baer, for the most part, centers around the subject of transformation promoting with a specific end goal to encourage his perusers or groups of onlookers in changing over their site activity into unadulterated deals. In the event that you are into promoting and have been searching for viable approaches to change over movement into deals, you should visit his blog and read his blog entries.

Best of all, he likewise covers content promoting methodologies that one can follow keeping in mind the end goal to construct the online group of onlookers through blog content without any preparation. In this way, on the off chance that you are searching for a genuine promoting master who can show you the rudiments and also give you approaches to transform activity going to your blog into deals, you should look at Jay Baer web journals and his book.

Pat Flynn

Congratulate Flynn initially entered the stuffed business in the time of 2008 with his blog "Savvy Passive Income." Even, however, this field was firmly pressed with contenders, he figured out how to make his blog productive rapidly with his diligent work and vision. Before entering the very aggressive promoting field, he used to work at an engineering firm.

It was his obsession and frenzy for progress that drove him this far. He set an alternate precedent in the market by truly sharing his wage reports and the ways and strategies through which he used to win the sum.

You will be amazed to realize that regardless he shares his wage reposts and due to his straightforwardness and reliability towards his perusers, his perusers love and regard him as well as purchase products from him. A huge piece of his salary originates from advancing subsidiary items that he underwrites and trusts.

He composes and shares certified item surveys to instruct his perusers about the associated items. He is a functioning individual via web-based networking media, and notwithstanding that, not at all like different advertisers, he shares the majority of the adaptation procedures that he utilized and found fruitful for building and growing an online business.

Jon Morrow

Jon Morrow is a genuine motivation for bloggers and has accomplished the outlandish in his life. Jon experiences Spinal Muscular Atrophy, and even with his inability, he has accomplished a noticeable position and regard in the web-based showcasing an industry that not very many have accomplished.

In 2013, Job Morrow established Boost Blog Traffic Blog, and not long after its dispatch, this

Legends and web-based social networking are for all intents and purposes excess. The online talk process runs wild, especially with regards to Instagram.

Arranging reality from fiction is an all-day job—specifically, Ken Watson's occupation. He works with different business people, independent ventures and expert relationship on their online networking showcasing from training to all-out media administration administrations.

Watson likewise runs #ChatGramLive, an Instagram visit appear. It gives the most recent data, updates and news about Instagram on his Facebook page.

He and deals and promoting master Aaron Kilby discussed busting Instagram bits of gossip and fantasies, beginning with whether Instagram presents ought to be restricted on four or five hashtags.

"No," Watson said. "This gossip began toward the start of the year in a blog entry. The blogger gave zero sources to this information. Utilizing just four or five hashtags on a post can have long-haul harming impacts; diminish likes or remarks; diminish adherent development; diminish reach; et cetera.

"Instagram permits up 30 hashtags per post, so bet everything," he said. "Have your center hashtags—12 to 15—you can use for each post, and the rest are theme particular for that post."

To back up his case, Watson noticed an AgoraPulse learn around 30 hashtags.

Numerous specialists or impacts say it's smarter to put hashtags in the main remark rather than in the inscription.

"I've generally told individuals and the records I run, put the hashtags in your Instagram post inscription," Watson said. "Gathering and place them off the beaten path in the base piece of the inscription.

"In the event that you put the hashtags in the primary remark for whatever reasons, you need them prepared to go immediately in your clipboard," he said. "At that point, you can glue them into the main remark. Time is the main consideration with hashtag execution."

AgoraPulse distributed another examination identified with this theme.

Out of the shadow forbidding

Watson said alleged "shadow prohibiting" on Instagram is exaggerated.

"It's solitary a thing since individuals still make it a thing," he said. "Instagram shadow prohibiting has turned out to resemble an urban legend of sorts, the Instagram Slender. Individuals see a drop off in commitment or reach and consequently bounce to the end they are being shadowed restricted.

"There are such a large number of components into what could cause an Instagram post to perform gravely," Watson said. "There's day or time, an awful blend of hashtags, and possibly the substance itself. I've needed to tell individuals your subtitle and hashtags were spots on, however, your content—well it just sucked. Individuals weren't associating with it, so they continued looking over."

Another Instagram fantasy fights that setting hashtags in histories helps profiles in inquiry rankings.

"Hashtags in your profile have zero effect on hunt rankings," Watson said. "The substance in your Instagram profile bio isn't accessible. He just the time you need a hashtag in your profile is if it's a grouped one and you need individuals to see content with that hashtag."

At regular intervals there appear to be posts saying the Instagram calculation has changed. Watson doesn't consider this to be a major factor.

"Generally, the Instagram calculation has remained the equivalent since it at first took off," he said. "There have been quite recently some minor changes all over. Nothing major has been done to it like we have seen over on Facebook with its calculation."

Boundless posts

In spite of another talk, Watson invalidates the thought that Instagram will just show presents on 10 percent of devotees.

"In no way, shape or form," he said. "Instagram doesn't conceal content. That is Facebook. Instagram's calculation is a need positioning framework. You control what you see.

"In the event that you like and remark on a record's substance as often as possible, the calculation will check that record as high need," Watson said. "On the off chance that you pursue a record and you don't connect with it, the calculation marks it low need."

Each activity has a continuous impact.

"Each time you open the application, it sorts with a blend from most astounding to least," Watson said. "In the event that you are dynamic with Instagram, in the long run, you will find in your feed an 'All Caught Up,' which implies you have seen everything throughout the previous two days."

There is likewise a false tie between Instagram Stories and the scope of primary feed posts.

"Generally, there is no association between the two," Watson said. "What's happening in Stories and what's happening in feed posts are two separate things.

"Your feed posts can get a little lift in reach with the new offer post to the Stories work," he said. "Be that as it may, don't share the majority of your presence on Stories. Offer the ones that are vital and you need your gathering of people to see."

Instagram business profiles likewise hold their rankings in the news source contrasted with individual profiles.

"Changing to a business profile has no negative effect at all," Watson said. "Instagram isn't Facebook. In the event that you been keeping down on exchanging over, don't keep down. Flip that change to your business profile."

On the off chance that there's one thing advertisers discover more difficult than whatever else, it's making Facebook promotions. With continuous calculation changes and not as much as perfect outcomes, numerous brands are quiet with regards to promoting along these lines.

These sorts of results can hose one's energy for making viable Facebook promotions, however considering the chance to connect with a lot of clients among your gathering of people it might surely be justified regardless of the exertion. Then again, enlisting promoting experts to create them for you may be the best approach.

Outsourcing your Facebook advertisements takes a ton of worry off of your shoulders, however, it could add a layer of hazard to the undertaking.

On the off chance that your promotion doesn't draw in your group of onlookers, in addition to the fact that you are passing up the potential income from your pitch, yet you will likewise be paying out cash for the advertisement and for the advertisers.

The whole circumstance can be befuddling, so it may appear to be certain that running Facebook promotions all alone is absolute franticness. Is it, however? With these tips, your advertisements could be more effective.

Spotlight on Your Offer

Time after time, brands are always improving their advertisement duplicate to check whether it will create better outcomes. What they don't understand, nonetheless, is that the promotion duplicate isn't the concentration for the normal customer. The talk there is imperative. You need to make a connecting advertisement on the off chance that you need to support change however much as could reasonably be expected, yet even a magnificently composed promotion won't have the capacity to beat an offer that doesn't constrain your gathering of people.

Your Facebook promotion should put your offer at the front line as the proposition ought to tempt in its very own right.

Add something to your offer that sweetens the pot whether it's giving to a philanthropy after a specific measure of offers or it's including reward swag. A straightforward rate off may draw the eyes of a few customers, however, they see comparable offers incalculable times each day, so your advertisement may not emerge.

Keeping in mind the end goal to really augment the impact of your offer, you'll need to blend great advertisement duplicate nearby it. Enlarge your offer with a duplicate that will summon the best possible feelings from your gathering of people. Spotlight on how they advantage. Expression you're offer so that it seems to be a support of your gathering of people instead of an ad to acquire your image benefit.

Track Sales

To legitimately expand and enhance your advertisement crusade, you have to sufficiently track your outcomes. There are many distinctive elements you can quantify, however, your most telling outcome will be dealt. Likes and offers aren't as great on the off chance that they're not transforming into deals. All things considered, the whole objective of Facebook advertisements is to support your change however much as could reasonably be expected.

Ensure you don't commit the normal error of accepting snaps will transform into deals. On the off chance that you see your promotion is in effect as often as possible shared, ensure you hold up to see the deals previously you announce it a win. You may need to improve your advertisement if it's being shared, yet you're not seeing the relating deals.

Offers and snaps are as yet vital measurements to gauge, however, income should dependably be your best need.

Plan For the Long Term

At the point when numerous brands approach Facebook promotions, they do as such expecting speedy returns that will in a split second prompt more income.

Online networking promoting is more confused than that. You need to assemble a fruitful promotion crusade as opposed to making a solitary successful advertisement. The best way to expand your change in a way that stays reliable is to continue refining your advertisements persistently to help transformation to an ever increasing extent.

While refining your advertisements may propose that you should test a few unique techniques, this shouldn't be done aimlessly. You have to build up a methodology for your testing and additionally for the battle itself. The subtle elements of this system will fluctuate a lot from industry to industry, so it will profit you to inspect what sorts of advertisements your gathering of people, for the most part, draws in with. To the exclusion of everything else, ensure you depend on the information. In the case of something doesn't work, quit doing it, regardless of whether you figured it would be a grand slam.

It's likewise vital to recall that losing some cash when first gaining a client is alright, and ensure you consider the client's lifetime esteem before you discount it as a misfortune. Losing cash toward the front is adequate when you remain to make a huge benefit as time goes on.

Perhaps It Is Insane

Staying aware of the majority of this yourself may be a madly difficult undertaking to begin. Picking the correct group of advertisers to fabricate Facebook promotions that will help support change, enabling your image to take off higher than ever can be overwhelming however required.

It's never too soon to start getting ready for what's to come. 2019 might just be a progressive year for SEO. Between virtual reality and expanded reality, or blockchain and man-made reasoning, we could see huge moves in the path we, as internet searcher analyzers, get things done.

Underneath we've assembled more than 15 of the business' best specialists to give their expectations on what we will see in 2019.

While there are numerous expectations that come as completely expected (indicate; the specialists put stock invoice look!), there are additionally a few, for example, Matt's or Yogesh's, that left the field.

This is what you can hope to see beneath:

Numerous specialists in the SEO business have made their forecasts for 2019:

Voice Search—According to 1/3 of SEO specialists voice hunt will be at the best for SEO patterns for 2019.

Versatile Focus—10% of specialists trust that portable will keep on commanding over work area in this way making improving for portable basic.

Blockchain—10% of specialists feel that blockchain will affect the manner in which that CEOs communicate with sites as far as specialized changes.

Amazon Search Optimization (AMSO)—is going to incline as indicated by 7% of specialists.

For the rest, you'll need to peruse on!

AI Is Going to Change How We Do Keyword Research

Jana Garanko, head of PR at the unbelievable promoting instrument, SEMrush, trusts that AI will change our catchphrase investigate practices, and rankings will rely upon private statistic information considerably more than they do now.

Computerized reasoning will turn out to be more omnipresent, so SEO authorities must handle firsthand information on machine learning and mechanization. A more prominent number of individuals will stick to voice seek, so SEO pros should change in accordance with this moderately new sort of inquiry. Since voice demands are not quite the same as would be expected inquiries, the watchword explore process is probably going to change.

While virtual reality advances begin conveying science fiction motion pictures to reality, I question that VR and AR will greatly affect SEO at any point in the near future. This involves years, however, and my figure is that in around 5– 10 years this sort of SEO will turn out to be more typical.

SERPs will get more customized and will consider clients' interests, leisure activities, area, seek history, and surely sexual orientation. Search engine optimization experts will likewise need to contemplate a more noteworthy measure of substance-related factors, for example, its length, quality, TF-IDF, and its structure.

As of now the greater part of looks represent cell phones, and the number will absolutely go up in 2019. Search engine optimization masters will keep on expecting to guarantee that their sites are portably agreeable. In addition, AMP will be on the ascent alongside new brisk SERP highlights.

Amazon Search and Voice Search Will Take Impressions Away from Your Site

Kent Lewis, President, and Founder of the Portland-based execution firm, Anvil, predicts that both Amazon hunt and voice inquiry will be inclined in 2019.

My forecast is that the greatest SEO drift in 2019 will be Amazon seek. 56% of shoppers start looks around items on Amazon (not Google), According to a Kenshoo contemplate. This is an enormous move that we're seeing and Amazon look can't be ignored. Amazon truly could be the new Google.

The second greatest SEO incline in 2019 will be voice look. The manner by which buyers seek to be recognizably changed by advanced aides.

At the point when shoppers look vocally, their questions are gigantically not the same as how they keep in touch with them out. The most perceptible part of this is voice seek produces some long-tail catchphrase questions. It will be a test improving for these terms. Do we make new pages to address each long-tail variety? Do we make a center page? The extra test that is additionally generally new is the idea of Position 0 on Google: answers to your inquiries at the highest point of the natural list items, above standard postings.

SEOs Will Put More Emphasis on Search Intent and Code Optimization

Beam Cheselka, SEO and AdWords Manager at SEO and plan organization, webFEAT Complete, predicts that destinations with over a two second load time will be punished, and look aim will keep on developing insignificance.

It's protected to state we are presently living later on. The greatest change that we'll see in 2019 (and that is now occurring) is that watchwords are ending up less imperative. Rather, the purpose behind a particular catchphrase or key phrase will wind up underlined further and advance by the ascent in versatile and voice seek.

For instance: Someone scans for "Most ideal approach to cook a turkey for Thanksgiving." That searcher likely is searching for strategies to cook a turkey, yet with every technique he/she might need to know why the strategy is ideal, how concentrated the procedure is, and what sort of turkey is best to purchase. As it were, we can do research and incorporate accommodating data with a substance that clients did not know they required. This better fulfills look expectation, supports commitment, and expands rankings.

To the extent new instruments, philosophies, and innovations go, there are a couple of things that ring a bell:

Information and Interpreting It :

Over the long haul, innovation will make it less demanding and less demanding to decipher the significance behind an inquiry question. This will prompt SEOs having the capacity to produce substance and offer guidance that obliges a substantially more particular group of onlookers and fulfills their necessities all the more totally.

Security :

As a greater amount of our lives occur on the web, it is just going to get more critical that sites are secure. This implies facilitating on secure servers, encoding our destinations, and staying up with the latest. Google as of now gives positioning lifts to destinations on a safe convention (https versus HTTP) and this accentuation on security will just develop over the long haul. Blockchain might just be the following emphasis of this.

Execution :

The cutting-edge client has a limited capacity to focus. On the off chance that a site takes in excess of a couple of moments to stack, she/he is probably going to clear out. Accordingly, it's extremely critical to ensure that site speed/stack time is enhanced however much as could reasonably be expected.

Advancements inside modules, the usage of CDN's, reserving systems, and key association of contents/CSS documents is at present successful. In any case, by 2019 a site stacking in more than 2 seconds could be punished. Google created AMP for a close momentary heap of sites when actualized appropriately, so we know execution is on their radar. Designers should take care of code, and really streamline JS/CSS and by and large HTML.

VR and AR Will Get Their Own Sections in Organic Search; Blockchain Will Create More of a Focus on Technical SEO

Yogesh Jain, organizer of India based computerized organization, Concept Allies, trusts that expanded and virtual reality and blockchain may change Google's natural hunt calculations.

Both virtual reality and increased the truth are promising advances for internet searcher promoting (both paid and natural). By 2019, the manner in which we inquiry probably won't change totally, however, these new advancements will change the manner in which we fabricate joins, draw in clients, and produce leads through substance promoting.

Content strategists are attempting emotional endeavors to fuse video into their plans. With AR and VR in the photo, they will definitely make sense of approaches to use these. AR and VR substance can likewise supplant the job of infographics in SEO. Additionally, Google as of now supports portable cordial sites. Since AR and VR are getting to be standard, Google may change their calculation to support destinations with more versatile commitment or perhaps think of another web search tool area concentrated just on AR/VR—just like what they have for pictures.

Concerning Blockchain, the effect will be resolved based on the size of appropriation. Seeing the present pattern, numerous organizations may consolidate blockchain and web 3.0 into their facilitating, in this way making it required for website admins to keep up locales on a specialized side with the goal that rankings aren't lost. The composition network is as of now attempting to make a markup for a similar reason.

Voice Search Will Make up Nearly half of Searches

Dave Gregory, Content Marketing Manager from the UK based execution promoting office, SiteVisibility, predicts that 2019, and not 2018, will be the genuine year of voice.

Voice look will be one of the primary regions of the center for SEO in 2019 and past. It's evaluated that by 2020, voice scan will represent around half of the aggregate quests and that effectively 40% of grown-ups at present utilize voice to look at any rate once every day. Inquiry advertisers will need to focus on how they need to catch this movement. As of now, we don't see many individuals concentrating much on it, so we believe that the brisk riser will get the worms.

It gives the idea that voice seek contains more words, as well as might be more focused on what a client is hoping to see. In this manner, practices, for example, making on page substance will require an alternate methodology. For instance, where already a garments organization could upgrade for 'Dark T-Shirts', they may now need to consider long tail inquiries, for example, "where is the least expensive dark shirt?"

We likewise think there will be significantly more plan to looks than there is as of now. Terms like 'where', 'how', 'why', 'when', and so on will all be included substantially more conspicuously. To put it plainly, we feel that SEO in 2019 should move concentrate considerably more towards noting individuals' inquiries and tackling individuals' issues. We additionally feel that as a beginning stage, the means taken by individuals to attempt and rank for included scraps will be a decent place to begin from to investigate voice look.

We think SEO in 2019 will see a move to concentrating much more on client purpose, critical thinking, and hyper area keeping in mind the end goal to benefit from the proceeded with the ascent of voice look.

Blockchain Is Going to Create New Movements in Search In 2019, online organizations will embrace more voice-to-content innovation to build commitment and inquiry action.

Visual hunt in light of commitment with pictures and camera information is a major chance to cultivate importance, maybe as right on time as 2019. A client should need to take a photo of a thing or condition with their telephone and tell the machine "I need this" and proceed onward with their day.

Counterfeit news" will be understood. Initiation attribution and verification will win the day, or clients will surrender channels with horrendous substance. Topic specialists will convey more weight after some time, and our devices will help our scan for dependable substance or wind up insignificant themselves. Blockchain has an extraordinary guarantee here.

Namelessness will turn into a premium. We've made our very own casings of news and data from importance and inclination settings on the web. The guarantee of the democratization for web-based distributing was to enable a more extensive voice and give a stage to the creators, yet the drawback has been acknowledged with melodrama originating from the vocal minority. The drama will dependably win, as we've advanced to give our regard for dangers. We will receive apparatuses to quiet personalization to permit more extensive perspectives. We will have a need to movement online at the time and be unhampered by our breadcrumbs. Blockchain has an extraordinary guarantee here too.

Versatile and Voice Importance Continue to Dominate

Caleb Backe, SEO Manager for Maple Holistics, composes that versatile and voice will proceed with their control of significance as we depend on work area less and less.

On the off chance that you need to recognize what sort of SEO patterns will create in 2019, look no more distant than the patterns that are creating in the hunt in both 2017 and 2018. We're long past portable inquiry and voice-seek being a 'trend'—they are the all-out ordinary currently, exceeding work area look in both volume and SEO-positivity.

In view of this, one can securely wager that SEO in 2019 will intensely support results that are the most versatile and voice-question benevolent. This implies organizations seeking rank for pursuit terms should center around giving absorbable answers, and in addition, offering their data in conversation starter/answer form—much a similar way one would ask Google over voice-look.

Also, as is dependably the case, internet searcher calculations will keep on winding up more complex. In 2019, you can wager that White Hat SEO will have isolated itself significantly promote from Black Hat SEO, and that to the exclusion of everything else, giving quality substance will be the most imperative factor for organizations positioning in pursuit.

Anticipate that User Experience will Increase in Importance

Chris Brantner, SEO Director at SleepZoo, trusts that UX will be the urgent SEO center in 2019.

In the course of the most recent 5 years, SEO has changed enormously, and I just anticipate that the pace will revive throughout the following couple of years.

So what will SEO look like in 2019?

I think client experience will turn out to be one of the biggest positioning elements. Google is pushing towards more customized list items, so with the end goal for you to perform well, you'll need to guarantee that you give a superior client encounter that keeps individuals on your site. You will require content that connects with them and a site that heaps extremely quick to shield them from hitting that back catch.

Social Channels Will See More Indexing and Social Media Optimization Will Be Very Important for Organic Search

Amy Kilvington, Marketing Executive at Custom Curtains, trusts that SEOs will need to upgrade web-based social networking more as Google lists it and organizes it over their destinations' pages.

By 2019, content advertising is set to wind up an industry worth $300 billion. It's implied that this will hugely affect website streamlining no matter how you look at it; all things considered, the two come as a couple.

We're expecting SEO without bounds to be considerably more substance and buyer centered. Sites will keep on delivering content that is made particularly for people, not simply the internet searcher. Brands will turn out to be more exploratory with the substance they share and the associations they hit up with influencers.

Internet-based life will likewise assume a major job in SEO without bounds. Social channels will keep on incorporating with pursuit, all in all, both as far as more substance being recorded and positioned by the web search tool (as Google as of now does with tweets from specific records), and clients using these social stages as a web crawler in its own right. YouTube is as of now the second biggest web search tool, recall!

Upgrade Other Platforms for Search in 2019

Joe Goldstein, Lead SEO and Operations Manager at Contractor Calls accepts too that SEOs should improve different stages for inquiry.

As Google's list items turn out to be progressively adapted and different stages, for example, Amazon and YouTube acquire SoV and pursuit volume, I believe we're late for the focal point of SEO to move far from Google. In time, the line between web-based life administration, channel advancement, and SEO will be fundamentally blurrier than it is today.

Obviously, there are a few factors that could accelerate, back off, or even turn around this development. YouTube adaptation has experienced enormous changes in the course of the most recent year which have made it troublesome for substance makers to depend on customary video adaptation, rather pushing them towards new alternatives like sponsorship and marked attire. Since Amazon has entered the physical space by means of the Whole Foods securing, Walmart has started to push into the web-based business space by offering answers for outsider merchants. It's additionally too soon to state what the long haul eventual fate of VR and brilliant speakers will be and whether both of them will materially affect hunt or media utilization.

Regardless of which stages have picked up or lost ground by 2019, we can expect that the ongoing flood of SEO positioning component studies will persist onto the most conspicuous stages. A developing comprehension of and access to huge information preparing implies an ever-increasing number of distributors will figure out those positioning elements, setting the stage for new instruments, brands, and complexity.

Area and Voice Search for More Hyper-Targeting

Teresa Walsh, Marketing Executive at vehicle site, Cazana, predicts that hyper-natural focusing on will expand its significance in 2019 with more area pursuit and more voice look.

Voice inquiry will change how we associate with web crawlers and it will make SEO considerably more focused and imperative to online achievement. The setting is essential to voice seek rankings. When we are looking through Alexa and Siri we are getting 1 output. This implies site proprietors and SEO specialists should be large and in charge with regards to watchword research and keeping the setting of their site pertinent to clients.

Over half of all web movement is by means of portable today and 76% of individuals who utilize area look visit a business inside one day. This number is colossal. Area look is developing each year and we are utilizing our cell phones day by day to scan for answers and arrangements locally to us.

Voice pursuit and area inquiry will turn out to be significantly more imperative.

Anticipate that Searchers will More Frequently Get Their Answers Without Actually Going to Your Website—SEO Real Estate Is Shrinking

In 2019, we will need to advance voice seek answers with CTAs that Google's calculations don't get on, yet people do. Dan Mallette, Lead SEO Strategist at both InVue Digital and HearstDMS, predicts that SEOs should streamline for voice inquiry and find new roads as SERP land contracts.

While the essentials of SEO will continue as before, the scene will keep on ending up increasingly aggressive in 2019. Google keeps on expanding fast data in the SERPs, from upgraded item data, extended audits, to answer boxes. This land offers need to brands and will just keep on extending as Google puts increasingly trust in substances as opposed to people.

Having the capacity to give clear, brief, and precise data will go up against more noteworthy significance with an ever increasing number of home colleagues hitting the market. Outside of business associations, voice look as of now puts an overwhelming dependence on the appropriate response confines seek. This puts a heavier onus on advertisers and brands to have the capacity to give answers to the inquiries clients are inquiring.

Before long, "being on the main page" won't be sufficient on the grounds that voice looks don't depend on pages. Having the capacity to answer questions over an expansive range of information will be basic as the piece of the overall industry for voice develops.

Computerized reasoning and Technical SEO Will Be the Trend in 2019

Chris Gregory, author and overseeing accomplice at Jacksonville based firm, DAGMAR Marketing, predicts that AI and machine learning will bring in the big affect SEO in 2019 and CEOs who aren't specialized will be left in the residue.

The eventual fate of SEO will include man-made reasoning, with the enormous players putting resources into machine learning. As only one case of how SEO is developing in this way, this colossal SEMrush ponder did not utilize connection investigation to land at their decisions. Rather, they utilized a machine learning calculation.

We are now taking note of how commitment measurements, for example, bob rate, time nearby, number of pages saw et cetera, are winding up to a greater extent a positioning element. This is the reason exceptionally valuable long frame content is compelling today; this kind of substance, when well done, normally makes individuals remain on the site longer. Google is utilizing man-made brainpower to mirror human commitment on locales and compensating destinations that showcase noteworthy measurements of ease of use. We presume that as a kneejerk response, a few people searching for fast wins will concentrate less on nasty external link establishment and more on discovering approaches to diversion commitment measurements.

It's anything but difficult to get diverted amid an online course.

Simply this week, I had a direct ordeal of what it feels like to be in the group of onlookers and simply have one such a large number of diversions.

Half a month prior, I had agreed to accept an online course from a teacher I truly appreciate: she was sharing bits of knowledge that were critical, as well as the planning was immaculate, and I have put resources into gaining from her. I checked the timezones, connected it to my timetable, and ensured I was prepared to go a couple of minutes before the begin time.

I was sat at the table in my kitchen, and I began to watch.

And keep in mind that she attempted her best to empower connection with us immediately with "Disclose to us where you are from in chatbox!" and "Fast survey: do any of you battle with this as well? Indeed or No?" … when I saw a pile of dishes out of the side of my eye, I felt constrained to rapidly wash them while tuning in.

At that point in an especially long monolog about the foundation for an up and coming point—I wound up making a speedy keep an eye on my Facebook, finding a couple of messages that totally should have been tended to, and keeping in mind that the program was open… a jump over to Gmail.

For most of the session, I blocked in and out, flipping from effectively tuning in to not notwithstanding being in the room by any stretch of the imagination.

At last, when my more youthful sister came in the life with a progression of inquiries regarding our plans for the night, I snapped my workstation close, revealing to myself I could get the replay, and just didn't return.

All in all, what occurred here?

How could I go from being effectively intrigued, anxious to get into the experiences of this expert—to being disengaged to the point that I stopped before the online course had even wrapped up?

It wasn't that the substance wasn't significant, it wasn't that I didn't locate her trustworthy.

Perhaps it was just that I was at home.

Also, when the gathering of people isn't in the life with the speaker, additional exertion must be ensured the group of onlookers remains locked in.

At the beginning of online courses, speakers would talk and gatherings of people would sit and tune in, however for current groups of onlookers, we don't share that equivalent core interest.

While an ever-increasing number of speakers bring their substance online by offering online classes, how might you remain in front of alternate speakers by getting innovative and intuitive in your sessions?

This article will jump into a couple of thoughts on how you can remain on top of things and give gatherings of people quality data while ensuring they remain drew in with you until the online class is finished.

Need a short outline of the primary themes this article covers? See the infographic beneath.

1. Get their riggings pounding: Exercises, difficulties, and break out gatherings

Sit out of gear hands are the… diversions… workshop.

At the point when your gathering of people is requested to be straightforwardly required with something that is going on, the shot that they will have meandering eyes is limited.

They'll additionally absorb more data on the off chance that they are effectively locked in. Contingent upon the length and nature of your substance, search for spots where you can add fragments of collaboration to supplement and develop the data you are giving them.

This could be as straightforward as "Record 3 things that [fill in] at this moment. Take 2– 3 minutes, and really record it." or as mind-boggling as part the whole crowd up into breakout rooms where they examine a theme and (Check if your stage gives breakout rooms: for instance Zoom underpins up to 50 breakout rooms with a maximum of 200 individuals for every room.)

On the off chance that you are sincerely busy recording something, you are most likely not going to look at what is going on Facebook.

Obviously, you can't influence your whole gathering of people to do the activities or difficulties, yet offering them will go far.

Activities that test and connect with your gathering of people will make your online class intelligent and fascinating, actuating their brains and expanding the estimation of your online course.

2. Be unconstrained

Much the same as a monotone speaker, in the event that you have a dull online class, regardless of how great the content—you'll battle to connect with your group of onlookers.

It's human instinct to get exhausted effortlessly and rapidly.

The cerebrum needs incitement to keep actuated, this is the reason dreariness is so exhausting to listen to—we comprehend what is coming up straight away, and our brains begin hunting down another thing to be keen on.

Along these lines, switch it up!

Routinely and spontaneously—if you continue astounding your group of onlookers, you'll keep them stuck to the screen.

While it might appear to be strange to design immediacy, the thought is that it appears to be unconstrained to the crowd.

Here are a few thoughts on the most proficient method to add suddenness to your online class:

Get amaze influencers and visitors

Expedite a powerful individual that you didn't declare.

This could be another driving master, a partner, a mainstream creator or expert colleague, yet an unexpected visitor can truly crest intrigue. Regardless of whether they remain for a couple of minutes to offer a key understanding, this can be extremely energizing for your group of onlookers and keep them reeled in.

For the guest—they will get the presentation to another group of onlookers, for a low time speculation.

You could even attempt pre-recording their piece beforehand and playing it amid the session on the off chance that they are not ready to make the particular time of your live chronicle.

2. Giveaways

Why not begin your online course off with a giveaway? You could even do numerous giveaways all through the session.

What might you be able to offer?

- Duplicates of your books,
- a free counsel,
- tickets to an up and coming occasion you are talking at,
- a membership to a confided in the new source,
- a perusing rundown of books that you could send them specifically from Amazon
- whatever is topical and significant to your group of onlookers, which you can fit into your financial plan.

While numerous online course have held off to the specific end to complete a wager, beginning with an impetus appropriate from the begin could make intrigue immediately

3. Pick an arbitrary group of onlookers part and work with them straightforwardly.

Rather than discussing things in hypothetical terms, pick a man aimlessly straightforwardly from your group of onlookers (or you could request a volunteer.) at that point feature your aptitudes, skill, or item specifically on them. For instance, they could experiment with your item and you could demo it, or in the event that you do counseling, counsel with them straightforwardly in front of the live gathering of people.

Regardless of whether it isn't 100% smooth (which can happen when working with somebody from the group of onlookers on a live chronicle) it is smarter to be somewhat harsh on the edges at that point to exhaust, and the gathering of people will take advantage of the sensing that they are watching something genuine and genuine than over cleaned and dry.

This being stated, keep these fragments on the shorter side, simply in case.

4. Moment surveys

When you are making your session, think of a bunch of surveys you could haul out whenever amid your session.

In the event that anytime, you feel like things are getting somewhat dry or that individuals may lose consideration, break out a survey and force the group of onlookers back.

A couple of the surveys can be only for the sake of entertainment, just to separate the substance and add greater suddenness to the session. Here are a couple of survey questions you could break out at pretty much any session:

On the off chance that you could go in time, okay need to see, the past or what's to come?

For what reason did you choose to join this occasion today?

Which superpower might you want to have?

In a single word, what's the best creation of the 21st Century?

Which open (or industry) figure is your own legend?

While you will need to keep the greater part of your surveys on the theme, and that includes esteem, despite everything you need to keep the online course as new and connecting as could reasonably be expected, so and a couple of fun inquiries can help.

3. Changes things up regularly

John Medina, a formative atomic researcher, and instructor at the University of Washington. says peer-checked on studies, and his own investigations and perceptions, demonstrate that our brains will unavoidably begin to get exhausted following a simple ten minutes.

He gauged the consideration of his understudies through the span of a 50-minute address, and saw that their advantage fell definitely after the initial ten minutes, and afterward grabbed again comfortable end of his address, in a swoop that looked something like this:

What's more, with every one of the diversions accessible to a group of people who isn't even in the stay with you, we can wager that the capacity to focus is considerably shorter when your gathering of people is on the web.

So what would it be advisable for you to do? Cutoff each online course to 20 minutes? Indeed, even that probably won't be successful.

Rather, center around recovering the gathering of people's consideration each seven to ten minutes by switching something up.

With the ten-moment resets, their advantage looks more like this:

When you are building your introduction ensure you are intentionally adding breaks and resets to keep consideration high

Presently, take note of that you would prefer not to switch it up more than this: it could start to appear to be disorderly, such as something out of Pee Wee's Playhouse. On the off chance that it's excessively difficult, making it impossible to remain on the indistinguishable page from you, they may lose the intrigue or get baffled.

Discover more concerning why you have to switch up your introduction here "Can you reconnect an exhausted group of onlookers?"

Skirt the monolog and switch the voice up. Here are 3 different ways to change up your introduction:

Hosts and different speakers

In the event that an online course has more speakers, it will offer various types of information—different perspectives, distinctive introduction styles, and obviously, unique voices.

Having a host, co-have or diverse visitor speakers can enable you to separate the consistency the main having one voice offers.

While you can at present be the superstar, as it were, every so often exchanging up the voice can offer an invigorating lift to sections and keep the gathering of people locked in.

Simply ensure whoever you are expediting knows their substance and is on the indistinguishable page from you to the extent the objectives of the online class and needs of the gathering of people.

APPLE

Apple is a brand, an iconic electronics device provider who seems to have lost their edge post the death of Steve Jobs. Steve was an innovator and a figure to look up to in any kind of dilemma. Without steve, apple seems to be stumbling to reach somewhere.

Apple could now take the time to reset their marketing strategies and rethink their plans once again but they might have to hurry up before their competitors make note of their current situation and try to hurriedly catch up with them.

Apple could reinvent their marketing strategy by repositioning the brand as a consumer-centric. All they would need to do is announce that they are going public with their development needs. i.e. they could go to their very own users and ask them what features would they most likely want in their iPhone next model and if they would like to help build it with them on a platform which is controlled by them alone. Being a brand Apple could quite easily create a stir in the market with most programmers now viewing this portal to see what ideas would users come up with. Apple could easily make this portal only accessible to internal employees and to those who submitted their entry with their visibility set to only their own entries to stop prying eyes from getting any new ideas.

Post this apple could internally form a team of their onBoard experts to lead a team of new programmers who would want to or take interest to develop a part or the whole solution. This would automatically create the stir in the public for the upcoming new Apple Phone and as well catch the much-needed media attention and all this without spending a single dime for marketing.

Now Apple could easily announce the launch of the phone on the same platform within the community who chipped in with their ideas to the same people acknowledging their ideas and as well appreciating the effort.

How Facebook could reset their marketing by repositioning their brand.

Facebook has always been a customer-centric and focused brand but they took some major beating a few months back due to their failure to safeguard customer data.

This has led to some major trash talk and even the most trending hashtag led by former WhatsApp CEO which was #facebookquit.

Facebook could soon double back with this simple strategy. Facebook has to realize that their core business was never data security and hence with a simple sorry could go under the Google Protect umbrella. As one of the strongest strengths of Google is security, Facebook could quite easily tie up with them and once and for all put an end to all the customer Woes and issues.

This would be a strategy that Facebook should go for which can reinvent their brand and bring back the confidence with undo the loss to the brand due to the data breaches.

How LinkedIn could Reset, Rethink and Reposition their marketing

LinkedIn though started as a social media platform for the executives but now has grown to a lot more than just that. Now LinkedIn has to realize that though it has bought Lynda.com, they never have actually turned it to their advantage to grow from a social platform. They need to reset their planning and reposition as a platform where professionals could learn together, gamify their learning and grow as professionals, ready to be taken for projects that companies may have.

They could quite easily let the professionals learn for free on their integrated Lynda.com platform and let them pay an extra fee for getting placement or projects to work on. This way LinkedIn could convert themselves into the first global platform to give trained and project ready professionals for any project. Thus they could definitely grow from there position now to a global Learning and Development center for working professionals where the professionals would have a location to show the recruiters their credentials with proofs and with experiences too.

This way LinkedIn could quite easily leverage their Lynda.com investment and grow globally for both organizations to seek business ready professionals and professionals for projects & which would normally not have been allowed to them. LinkedIn could quite easily turn out to be the best consulting organization with experienced and project ready resources.

How Twitter could change their strategy by resetting their marketing and repositioning their brand.

Though Twitter has now grown to be a global brand for sending short social messages, they still lack the killer edge which brands like Facebook, Snapchat and others had from the way go. Now, it is high time for Twitter to realize that and hence take into account some changes to reset their basic marketing and sharing fashion.

Twitter could reposition their brand by understanding that the user perspectives have changed and now they would like to be specific to one locality then share the same message globally. So Twitter should work on bifurcation of their user accounts based on Locality or region. This would help their customers share a simple tweet to a local community whereas they could share a different message globally as a brand.

This simple but effective upgrade would make Twitter go a long way as a brand which has now opened its platform for its customers to assist them target and be focussed to customers. They could relapse this based on the market demand and the demand for localization.

Book Reviews

Rashmi - 2 Years of Experience in Marketing + 1 year Experience in Engineering

**Current Position - Assistant Marketing Manager
Qualification - B Tech in Electrical Engineering**

The book by Krishna Avancha 'Reset, Rethink, Reposition' focuses on the trending marketing strategies and their implementations. Modern marketeers often don't know what it was like to market in the past. The ideas then were more idealistic, natural and spontaneous with no metrics to track the customer satisfaction, retention or growth. This book ensures that you relive the 'Age of Restoration' with practical examples from the industry because in Marketing, the success of the enterprise depends largely on creating a convincing illusion. Krishna Avancha rises to this challenge with great skill in this accomplished, atmospheric and thoughtful book.

Shruti - 4+ Years of Experience in Web and Graphic Designing

Current Position - Graphic Designer
Qualification - BA Economics

With 10 years of experience in Sales and marketing, Krishna Mohan Avancha has carved a niche for himself and has his own entourage rightly earned through his life as a marketeer. His book contributes to the raging demand of Digital Marketing and is a treat to the marketeers who like to swim against the tide and envisage history. As it is not always that you get to pounce upon a chance to learn from such elite personalities, I think the book could have included more practical examples.

Rasika - 5+ Years of Experience in Digital Marketing

Current Position - Digital Marketing Executive

Qualification - B Tech Computer Engineering

I liked this book. People who are interested in modern trends of marketing as well as those seeking career in marketing will most probably be interested in reading this book. Readers can gain knowledge of what it was like to market in the early years of evolving Digital Marketing. One of the things that was especially interesting is that there were practical examples considered and presented with thorough research and facts. Also, a big contrast between the then and now of marketing is discussed which explains how you can target your audiences. This book is very well written and useful for building your business strategies.

www.ingramcontent.com/pod-product-compliance
Lightning Source LLC
Chambersburg PA
CBHW020659220526
45464CB00001B/500